Caught in the Middle: Children of Divorce

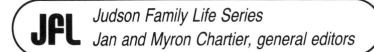
JFL Judson Family Life Series
Jan and Myron Chartier, general editors

Caught in the Middle: Children of Divorce

Velma Thorne Carter and J. Lynn Leavenworth

Illustrations by Daniel Panachyda

Judson Press ® Valley Forge

CAUGHT IN THE MIDDLE: CHILDREN OF DIVORCE

Copyright © 1985
Judson Press, Valley Forge, PA 19482-0851
Second Printing, 1987

Bible quotations in this volume are from the Revised Standard Version of the Bible copyrighted 1946, 1952 © 1971, 1973 by the Division of Christian Education of the National Council of the Churches of Christ in the U.S.A., and used by permission.

Library of Congress Cataloging in Publication Data

Carter, Velma Thorne.
    Caught in the middle.

    (Judson family life series)
    Bibliography: p.
    1. Children of divorced parents—United States.
2. Divorce—United States. 3. Divorced parents—United
States. I. Levenworth, J. Lynn. II. Title.
III. Series.
HQ777.5.C37 1985   306.8′9   84-21307
ISBN 0-8170-1037-8

The name JUDSON PRESS is registered as a trademark in the U.S. Patent Office.
Printed in the U.S.A. ⊕

To

Nancy, Nick, Debbi, Celia,
Mary Beth, Jamie, and Caroline
who survived our parenting

Acknowledgments

The authors would like to acknowledge the many people who have been helpful in the writing of this book. Jean Billings, Dr. Richard Josiassen, and Dr. Thurman Booker, our able colleagues who have engaged us in critical evaluation and shared their own insights and experience. We are indebted to Sandra Brucker for prodding our slow-moving pens and for her organization and efficiency in typing the final draft of the manuscript.

Above all, we acknowledge the support and education we have received from that stream of single-parent men and women with whom we have worked over the years.

Finally, we express our gratitude to Drs. Jan and Myron Chartier, the editors of this series, without whose encouragement this book would not have been undertaken.

V.T.C. and J.L.L.

Editors' Foreword

Caught in the Middle: Children of Divorce, by Velma Carter and Lynn Leavenworth, makes a significant statement to divorced persons who have the responsibilities of parenting their children. This book is one volume of a series of books published by Judson Press on marriage and family for contemporary Christians. The purposes of the Judson Family Life Series are to inform, educate, and enrich Christian persons and inspire them:

a. to become acquainted with the complex dynamics of marriage and family living;

b. to pinpoint those attitudes, behavioral skills, and processes which nurture health and wholeness in relationships rather than sickness and fragmentation.

c. to consider marriage and family today in light of the Judeo-Christian faith.

As editors of the Judson Family Life Series, we are committed to make available the latest in family-life theory and research and to help Christian families discover pathways to wholeness in relationships. Every attempt will be made by the authors to apply new insights to the realities of daily living in marriage and the family.

Volumes in the series will focus on the stages of marriage, divorce, and remarriage; parenting; the black family; and nurturing faith in families. Each book will be designed to deal with specific issues in marriage and family living today.

In reading *Caught in the Middle: Children of Divorce*, you will soon encounter the vast experience of the authors whose lives have intersected literally hundreds of persons who are either single parents or who work to help single-parent families adjust and live life fully and productively. When we contacted Velma Carter and Lynn Leavenworth to write this volume, their response was both serious and enthusiastic. "We have learned so much, it will be a good opportunity to write our ideas down to be shared," they declared. Those who read the book will be the beneficiaries of their accumulated wisdom.

Velma and Lynn, along with their spouses, are founders of Reach Associates, a nonprofit, nonsectarian organization which began in 1972. Their primary function is to offer professional help for people when life is particularly difficult because of broken relationships or the need to deal with great changes. Their work has focused on improvement of family relationships; individuals who are alone after divorce, separation, or death of a spouse; couples who are preparing for marriage or remarriage; single parents, both custodial and noncustodial. They also provide training for professionals who want to improve their skills in working with people. Because of the increasing number of broken relationships in our culture and the depth of need for help, Reach Associates has consistently continued to grow. Its impact has been substantial.

We want to affirm the many faith dimensions that permeate this book. While overt religious discussions are to be found in only two or three chapters, we believe that each page speaks in a profound way to what it means to be children of God seeking for qualitative, responsible, whole relationships in the fragmented context of today's world. The practical suggestions undergirded by life experience and solid theoretical understandings are given that persons—parents and children—might experience restored wholeness in the midst of brokenness and fragmentation. You will find chapter study questions for reflection and discussion at the end of the book.

It gives us great joy to present to you Carter and Leaven-worth's book on responsible single parenting.

Jan and Myron Chartier
Eastern Baptist Theological Seminary
Philadelphia, Pennsylvania

Contents

Preface

Margaret Deland in 1910, writing with a pen dipped firmly in irony, expressed her critical concern for what she perceived as consequences of the emergence of new forces astir in the American society:

> Look! The heavens and earth and waters that are under the earth are yours! The song that the morning stars sing is for your ears. The eternal tides of life await your adventurous prows. The very winds of God are blowing for your sails! "You—*you*—YOU—," the higher education cries, "never mind other people, make the most of your own life. Never mind marriage, it is an incident; men have proved it so for themselves; it is just the same for women. Never mind social laws, do what your temperament dictates—art, affairs, enjoyment even. But do your duty to yourself!"*

She might have added, with more cold irony, "and never mind the children, just be true to yourself!"

---

*Margaret Deland, *Selections from 119 of the Atlantic*. Ed. by Louise Desaulniers (Boston; Atlantic Monthly Company, 1977), p. 246.

The tide of society sweeps on, and we would place this slender volume of words before that tide of events, saying, "Stop, look, and listen to the children." After all, it is the children of today who will be the shapers of the twenty-first century, practicing then what they are now learning in the living laboratories of human relations: the families in which they are now living. Of such is the hope of the kingdom of God!

Introduction

Raising children has never been easy. Each generation has its doomsayers, who proclaim "this is the worst of times," and its optimists who are sure "this is the best of times." All parents have their moments of panic and despair, of uncertainty and pain. At other times their children provide moments of satisfaction, tranquility, and unequaled joy. When there are two loving parents in the home, both sharing the heavy responsibility for the well-being of their children, there is a measure of security: someone to help in decision making, someone to give relief in caring for a sick child, someone to help bear financial responsibility, someone who can share in those big and little moments of joy. In homes where the marriage is working well (though the number of such homes is said to be decreasing), there is a sense of joint purpose, there are partners who give and receive love from each other, and thus the resources for nurturing their children are enhanced.

The parent who is raising children alone, particularly the divorced parent, has such an enormous task that it is no wonder he or she often feels overwhelmed. In addition to the problems faced by all parents, the custodial parent may be struggling with a damaged self-image, with grief, with anger, with depression, with feelings of failure, and with the difficulties of starting over. Almost all single parents must work full time and have complete care of home and family. They may be in the process of settling the legal issues connected with divorce—property settlement, custody of the children, financial support, child care for the working parent. These matters are not only time consuming, they are also emotionally and physically exhausting.

The parents have the children's emotional upheaval to deal with also, for the adjustment period is painful for the children. They may feel responsible for the breakup of the marriage; they may be angry and feel abandoned by one parent and worried about the possibility of losing the other. Nearly all children, given a choice, would prefer to have their parents together, and they often perpetrate elaborate schemes to try to bring them back together. Visitation with the other parent is a source of continual problems. Children get caught in a loyalty bind, unable to move closer to one parent without risking disloyalty to the other.

Then there is the role of the noncustodial parent. Little has been written about this person's role in the life of the children and the very real pain experienced in separating from the children. Noncustodial parents play an important part in the well-being of their children and in the effectiveness of the custodial parent. Regardless of the bitterness that may be present between parents, it is vital that the noncustodial parent be concerned for the parent who cares for the children. Noncustodial parents can reduce the tensions and deepen their relationship with their children. Much maligned by some custodial parents, these other parents can make the difference in how successful the divorce can be for all concerned.

Over the past ten years of working with single parents, we have listened to thousands of custodial and noncustodial parents. Most of them, we have found, are determined to do a good job in raising the children. They have overcome some incredible difficulties and have given unselfishly of themselves in most admirable ways. Some have expended themselves for the children to such an extent that they have nothing left for themselves. Of course there are those who, depleted, have lost the motivation and the energy to cope with the children and thus have left the children to parent themselves. This withdrawal robs the children of their childhood. Fortunately, these parents are very much in the minority.

Our experiences with single parents have enriched our lives. They have taught us about courage and the toughness and endurance of the human spirit. They have shown us that children can survive the trauma of divorce and that they and their parents can put their lives back together and move on without the psychological damage so often predicted. We believe the courage, the vision, the insights, the resourcefulness, the experiences, and the accomplishments of single-parent families constitute a rich resource for American society. Those who work their way through brokenness and pain gain knowledge of inestimable value in understanding the nature of love.

We want to share with you some of the experiences of these people, though of course we will not use their names.

The problems we discuss are not simple ones, and they do not yield to simple answers. We have no magic formulas, and we do not believe there is any quick and easy way to raise children even under the best circumstances. Yet we want to place before you insights and challenges that may be helpful to your family. We may ask you to do things that seem difficult for you. Only you will be able to judge your ability to carry through the suggestions given, but if you are willing to expend the effort necessary to get at the deeper issues at stake in some of the problems, we believe this book can provide useful, practical guidance. We have tried to be realistic in approaching these complex issues in order to provide you with resources for setting reachable goals of promise to yourself.

Our clients have reinforced our own conviction that one's faith is a resource of first importance in times of stress. They have told us of the part that faith has played in their ability to withstand the pressures of the divorce process, and they have, in many cases, come through it all with their faith not only intact, but also deepened. We have pointed to a variety of resources, and many more such resources may be found in the books listed in the bibliography we have provided.

We conceive of this book as an extension of the conversations we have had with the gathering company of men and women and their families who have moved forward to abundant living.

Like the legendary phoenix, they have risen out of the ashes of broken relationships to begin again.

1

The Marriage Is Over

The manner in which couples come to the realization that their marriage is over or in serious trouble differs widely. For some the awareness is a gradual process, as in a long terminal illness. The partners begin to spend more and more time in separate pursuits; their sex life diminishes in quantity and quality; they talk less and less about anything important; they don't enjoy each other any more; there's no excitement when they meet. For others the end comes with such suddenness that it shocks and terrifies one or both of them.

"What about the kids?" she screamed. "Who is going to take care of them, what am I going to do if one of them gets sick in the middle of the night? Have you thought about them, or can you think about anything besides yourself? How can you do this to me after all these years?" The words poured out of her, and her voice took on the shrill tones of panic. Genuinely concerned for the children, she was partly crying out for herself.

Jim tried to calm his wife. He admonished her about waking the children and frightening them. Wearily, he said, "Caroline, I don't know why this is such a surprise for you. Our marriage has been over for a long time; you simply haven't been willing to look at it. I have tried to tell you so many times, but you wouldn't hear. You preferred to pretend that everything was fine."

Jim and Caroline Taylor sat in the counseling room recounting the events of the past week. Her eyes were red, and she looked distraught, still not willing to believe what Jim had told her that night.

"I think he's sick," she said. "Something has gone wrong inside his head. There's nothing wrong with our marriage. We have three beautiful children, and he'd have to be crazy to want to give up everything we have worked for. If he'd only listen to reason, I'm sure there is nothing wrong that we can't work out."

"Why don't you tell them the truth?" Jim interrupted. "You know we haven't had sex for a year; we never do anything together. We fight all the time; we're like two strangers occupying the same house. I don't know what happened, but I do know that I don't love you anymore."

Jim and Caroline had been married for fifteen years. At the beginning of the marriage Jim was working on a graduate degree and Caroline had continued her job in order to support them while Jim studied. They had agreed that as soon as he finished school, she would stop work and they would start their family. They now have three children: a daughter (eleven) and two sons (nine and seven). Jim was employed as the comptroller of a small manufacturing company, earning a comfortable living. He worked several nights a week, even more at times, and often brought work home on weekends.

Caroline was content to stay at home with the children, but she had little energy for outside involvements. Jim, on the other hand, enjoyed playing tennis, jogging, and other sports, and he liked to socialize with people from the office. He often expressed the wish that they could do more entertaining. Gregarious, Jim liked to be the center of attention at parties, while Caroline found it hard to be at ease with strangers. Their arguments usually started over differences in how they should spend their free time. Caroline wanted Jim to take more interest in the family, be willing to work on fixing up the house, and simply to have fun with the children.

"Her whole life is those kids," Jim explained. "I love them, too, but I think there's more to life than raising kids. First thing you know, we'll be just like her parents. The kids will be grown, and we'll be sitting around waiting to die. Now when I have time off from work, I want to enjoy myself, and there was a time when she did, too."

They came to us too late for counseling to help. Jim had made up his mind to get out of the marriage. He had agreed to come only because he hoped it would help Caroline. She was so frightened by the thought of being alone that she couldn't even talk about divorce. She was very protective of the children, and she agreed to bring them to a second session only if the counselor would agree not to mention the word "divorce."

As is often the case, the children already knew that things were bad between the parents. When the counselor asked the eleven-year-old daughter, Amy, if she worried about her parents, she waited a long time before replying. Finally, with tears welling in her eyes, she said, "I'm afraid they are going to get divorced."

This same scenario gets played out in most homes where the marriage is in deep trouble. Even when both parties are aware that they have serious problems, one or both are often unwilling to face the truth. The prospect of divorce is too scary.

"How can I raise three kids alone?" she asked. "He can't afford to support two homes, and I can't imagine leaving these kids in someone else's care. We don't have any relatives nearby, or anyone else whom I could trust to take care of them." With her anger rising, Caroline flung bitter words at Jim, accusing him of everything from infidelity to insanity.

The terror that Caroline felt at the prospect of Jim's leaving is not hard to understand. With no family to give her support, she knew that the road ahead would be a very difficult one. She felt helpless, abandoned, and betrayed. She needed someone to guide her through the difficult months ahead; she had to deal with her own emotions as well as the children's. She had hard decisions to make; she had a lot of changes to face for herself and for the children, and the stress of change was already affecting her.

Jim had made up his mind, and there was no turning back. But for him, too, there were difficult days ahead. He had struggled for a long time over the idea of leaving the children. He had been raised in a one-parent family, and he knew what it meant for children to lose one of their parents. He remembered how he had cried during the long nights after his parents were divorced.

Support structures were needed for the whole family. There were so many short- and long-range problems to face. They had to deal with their emotions as well as some very practical problems. Competent legal advice was needed, and they had to call on resources from within their families and among their friends to help them get through it all. In fact, they found that they needed some professional counseling in order to work through all of the tangled difficulties. In their case they opted for counseling for the whole family, though others sometimes choose to seek individual counseling or choose not to involve the children.

Understanding What Has Happened

It was clear that Jim was unwilling to work on a marriage that he considered had not existed for a long time, but he came to see that it was beneficial to both of them to spend time in understanding how they had reached this point of separation in their marriage. We feel that this process can be very important for couples contemplating divorce. In the first place, it provides a structure in which they can talk to each other in a controlled setting, and perhaps learn to communicate at a deeper level than they had ever experienced before. Without understanding each other's side, it would be almost impossible to clarify and work on the issues before them.

Of course, there are times when one spouse may be more responsible for the breakup of a marriage than the other, but generally there is responsibility on both sides, and this kind of discussion can help each of them to see their own part in the relationship. The communication in itself provides a measure of healing, and it better prepares them for explaining to the children why the marriage has ended. If, on the other hand, they face the children with scapegoating and bitterness, they will place an unbearable, undeserved, and unnecessary burden on the children.

Another advantage of this kind of reflective discussion is that it helps the two people to understand themselves and their own needs better. In order to avoid a repeat of the same experience in later relationships, they need to understand what happened to the one in which they were, enabling them to be ready to start early in the next relationship to establish new patterns of relating.

While we never use this kind of counseling session to attempt to coerce partners to stay in a marriage, it sometimes does make them more aware of each other's needs and better able to deal with them, and occasionally a couple will decide to try again. If they do, we urge them to stay in counseling long enough to ensure their success in staying together. An on-again, off-again kind of marriage is much more damaging to children than a clear-cut decision to separate.

Supporting the Children

No matter how painful the situation, children prefer to have their parents together, and they will exert great pressures to try to keep them from divorcing. Children can behave in bizarre ways to influence their parents. They may start having temper tantrums, disobeying rules, and getting into fights in the school yard; they may start resisting the whole idea of school, kick and scream and even vomit to keep from going out the door when the bus comes. They can become physically ill to make sure that the parents will agree at least on one thing: the need to care for their child. Depending on the age and the personality of the child, the reactions vary; the kinds of support they need will have to be tailored to fit the needs. All the assurances the parents can give that they love the child are needed. They should be prepared to tell the child as clearly as possible what is going to happen. For most children, the immediate fear is "What's going to happen to me?" These frightened kids need to know how often they are going to see the departing parent, where they are going to live, and, if possible, they should be told that they can contact the noncustodial parent when they feel the need. We will discuss more fully in the next chapter the matter of telling the children.

Support for the Adults

In a time when divorce and separation are so common, it seems hard to understand why people are so reluctant to talk about it. Apparently driven by shame, couples are often hesitant to tell their friends, their family and others—the very ones in a position to give them support. "It will kill my parents; I simply can't tell them," we hear people saying over and over. "My sister has so many troubles of her own that I can't burden her with mine." To get at this reluctance, we sometimes ask our clients to imagine how they would feel if they had a grown-up child who was hurting deeply, but who held back from telling his or her parents in order to protect them. It is rare that we find anyone who says, "I wouldn't want to know about it." One of the hardest things for parents of grown-up children to face is the fact that their children no longer need them. Letting parents know that you are suffering greatly and that you need their love and assistance gives them an opportunity to help you in appropriate ways, and it increases their feeling of usefulness.

We use the word "appropriate" because it is important that you not let them become a crutch that will put you back in a dependent position where they make the decisions, even the rules for you. In this situation you become a child again, not an adult. You have real opportunity in the midst of your pain to grow, to learn to do things you never thought you could do, and to increase your self-esteem in the process. But parents can appropriately provide love and care for you and the children; perhaps they can provide assistance with child care on a temporary basis; they can help you to think through decisions that you have to make and possibly direct you to the professional help you need.

Friends are in a difficult situation. You should tell them what is happening to the marriage as soon as possible, and though you will be tempted to expect that they will take your side, you need to understand that it will be hard for friends who care about both of you. Allow them to "be there" for you without impairing their friendship with your partner. They can do this by spending time with you when you are feeling lonely, by letting you vent your anger and frustration and even by encouraging you to do so without having to agree with you. They can also take you to the movies, find helpful books for you at the library, take your kids for the day, or they can do dozens of other kind things that will let you know you are loved. And if they do the same for your partner, you should try to understand their caring without resenting it. Sooner or later they probably will lean toward one partner more than the other; but at the beginning making such a choice is so painful that if pushed, they will tend to withdraw from both of you rather than to be caught in the middle.

Friends can be very helpful in providing support for the children. If they ask how they can help, give them a chance to take the children for an outing or to do other simple things that will be genuinely supportive of the family. You can find ways to repay their caring when you have had time to recover. Don't wear them out, however; nobody wants to be around someone who is playing the same sad, bitter record over and over. Find some way to help your friends feel glad that they have seen you. Simple things like a thank-you note for "being there for me," or some homemade pastry or bread—something that costs you very little, but gives back to someone who cares for you—will help to keep the balances even.

The best thing about having a friend who will listen is that it takes the burden off the children. This kind of venting with adults is a way to ensure that you won't fall into the trap of asking your children to parent you. They deserve to be parented, not to be drawn into the parenting function themselves. This is not to say that you should hide your feelings from the children. It is important for them to know that you can talk about your feelings, because it gives them permission to talk about theirs. They need to know that both their parents are troubled by feelings of sadness. How else can they understand that a broken relationship is painful even when the adults involved have agreed to it?

Once the decision is made that you are going to separate, both partners should seek legal counsel. Even in states where it is legally permissible, to share an attorney we feel strongly that in the long run you will be better off to have separate counsel, at least in the beginning. You may later decide to engage the services of a divorce mediator in settling your property division, and in that case probably one attorney can handle the divorce in no-fault states. The savings in fees is considerable, but you want to be sure both of you have had equal rights represented.

Almost every community has counseling services available. If you are unaware of these resources, ask your family physician for a recommendation. Above all, don't hesitate to reach out for the help you need in the days when you really need it. There are many people who are willing and able to be of help.

There may be times when you doubt your own sanity. The events you have to deal with may be so difficult, your anger so great, and your confusion so total that you think you must be crazy. It may even feel to you as if no one else has ever gone through this before. Every situation is unique, but most separations bear similarities, and for this reason it will help if you can find somebody who has been through it all who is willing to give you help. Ask your pastor for the name of someone who has had a similar experience, then ask that person for a time to allow you to talk about what is happening. It is a gift to others to let them know they can help. While a person is helping you, he or she is also being helped. Married friends are important, but they may have to become your "daytime friends." Their presence may keep you from accepting the fact that you are single; they may be threatened by you (feeling their spouse may find you too attractive); or being in a "couples' world" may make you feel more lonely. When you have recovered enough to want adult companionship, you may have to seek out some new friends who are single.

Finding help for yourself has a direct relationship to the ability of your children to survive the trauma of separation and divorce. Usually the children will make it if the parents do. They are entitled to have parents who have not lost totally the capacity for fun and enjoyment. They begin to understand that life can go on and can be worthwhile, even though there are difficult things to bear.

Confusing the Children

One of the more difficult things for children to understand when their parents separate is indecision on the part of the parents, and also the tendency for the parents to say one thing and act out the opposite. Father announces that he is leaving, and then he either doesn't leave or he keeps coming back frequently for short stays—to pick up things he forgot or to fix this or that in the house. He may even stay overnight, sharing mother's bed. He's included in holidays, and everyone pretends that nothing has changed. Every time the departing parent returns, it raises hopes in the children that he or she is going to stay, and they have to go through the painful separation all over again.

When the departing parent finds it hard really to separate, there may be some important underlying cause. She or he may have some unfinished business in the marriage or may not be sure that separation is what the other person really wants. If this is the case, some third-party help should be sought to assist one or both of the parties in exploring whether or not there is any hope for the marriage to continue. Otherwise, we feel that it is better for the children if they have a clear-cut understanding that a firm decision has been made.

In most cases we feel strongly that visitation with the non-custodial parent should take place away from the home. This arrangement may be difficult with very young children, but it has many advantages. The children can begin to build a new relationship with the parent without feeling disloyal to the custodial parent. Also the custodial parent can begin to build a new life for himself or herself without fear of interference by the spouse. Visits away from the home permit some measure of privacy, so that the custodial parent doesn't have to fear criticism from the spouse for how she or he is running the household. Chiefly, however, it helps the children face the reality of their changed situation.

Handling Fears

When one parent leaves, children often worry that their other parent will leave, too. For this reason, they need constant reassurance that they are loved and that the remaining parent will not leave them alone. The departing parent can help tremendously with this kind of problem by telling the children that she or he will continue to be available to them and by making sure that such promises are carried out.

Children will sometimes express their fears of abandonment by wanting to sleep with the parent, either with the one who remains or when visiting the departed parent. Sleeping with the child is an easy habit to fall into, both because the child has real fears and the parent wants to comfort the child, or because of guilt on the parent's part that she or he has caused the child's problem, and because the parent also may enjoy the company and comfort of the child.

Reading to the child, hugging and holding, and talking quietly together for a time about the problem are all fine. But there should be no compromise in taking the child back to his or her own room, own bed, for sleep. You must establish early that life will continue as closely as possibly to the normal pattern, and any departure from your own determination will signal the child that you are wavering in your sense of what is best.

Aside from the sexual implications of having the child in your bed, there are other considerations for the future. You may one day decide to remarry, in which case you will have someone else in your bed, and that will mean that your child will feel replaced and rejected by you, causing the child further unnecessary anxiety. Holding a firm line is not an easy task— children can be very appealing, they can wear down your resistance, and they know exactly where to apply the pressure. While we have heard the story from dozens of single parents, Sandy's story is typical.

> My Jimmy won't give up. I tried for a long time to convince him that he should stay in his own bed, but he begged, cried, screamed about his fears of being alone. He would agree to sleeping in his own bed, but then in the middle of the night he would come into my room and sneak into bed with me. He got so clever about it that I didn't even wake up, but I would find him there the next morning. When I tried to punish him, he only got more hysterical about it, and I finally gave up. He has been sleeping with me now for over a year, and I know I'm stuck with him. I must admit that on a cold night he is a good snuggler.

It took a long time, but we were finally able to convince Sandy that she could actually change the situation if she made up her mind and if she were convinced that it was better for Jimmy to be in his own bed. When she decided that the time had come, she was surprised how easy it was. It took about a week of effort—of taking him firmly in hand—but then the battle was over. She made sure that there was a light in the hallway, she gave him a flashlight to have by his bedside, and she assured him that if he needed her she would come to him, no matter what the hour. The first few nights Sandy didn't get a lot of sleep; but when Jimmy saw her determination, he gave up the fight and began to sleep through the night peacefully.

You're the Expert

No one has better judgment about your kids than you do. You know your children better than anyone else, and you care about them more than anyone else. No one is more expert on the subject of your family than you are. You may need or want to seek outside advice. We all need to use all of the resources we can. But ultimately you have to evaluate what others tell you and make a decision based on your own knowledge.

Everybody makes mistakes in raising children. We often wish we could do it over, and we feel certain that we could do a better job than we did the first time. But we have to learn to accept the fact that we did the best we could with the tools we had available at the time. If we can say that with integrity, there need be no guilt.

Most children survive their parents' mistakes. Most even learn to forgive their parents' mistakes, especially after they grow up and have children of their own and see how difficult it is to raise children and to know always what is right.

It is important for you to believe in yourself, to trust your own instincts about the decisions you are making. Read all you can about what other people have to say regarding difficult parenting situations, but then apply it to your own family in a way that makes sense to you.

It may be hard for you to see it right now, but you are in the midst of what is essentially a "growth spurt." You are learning that you have strengths you didn't know you had. You are becoming more independent, and by doing so you are helping your children to see a whole different side of you. In spite of all the pain you are going through, the positive side is that as you analyze the mistakes you have made you will be able to change the patterns of your own behavior that are negative, and you can learn how to avoid making the mistakes again.

We would be amiss not to mention the possibility that all of the changes and their accompanying stresses could leave you feeling as if the whole world is caving in on you—that you are overwhelmed. If you begin to feel that you can't handle the situation, you owe it to yourself and your children to reach out quickly for professional help. The last thing your children need is to have you, too, abandon them through mental breakdown or self-destructive acts.

2

Telling the Children

We don't believe in keeping family secrets. There is nothing more dreadful than what children can imagine might be happening. They are like barometers; they can feel tension in the air. They don't even have to hear their parents fighting to know that things are not going right. And their imaginations work overtime about the meaning of what they feel.

Children notice small things—the fact that you don't talk much to each other, that when you do talk the answers are clipped and factual. They notice that Mother's eyes are red in the morning, they notice that you stop talking when they come into a room, or they notice when you are on the telephone with grandparents that they are not allowed to stay near the telephone.

Children are aware of symbols that you may not think they notice, such as Daddy no longer sleeps with Mommy, Daddy stays out very late at night, and Daddy doesn't call when he is going to be late for dinner. Their little computer minds begin to work overtime. In today's world, there are so many families breaking up and so much about divorce on television that children are much more attuned to the whole idea of divorce than any previous generation. They notice the little things.

In order to try to reduce the anxiety of your children, we think it is best to let them know what is happening in your relationship, at least in general terms, when there is trouble brewing. For example, if you and your spouse have decided to seek marriage counseling, it would be best for the children to know about it. You might want to say to them, "Mommy and I have been having a lot of problems lately, and we have decided to try to get someone to help us work out some solutions." It's good for the children to hear that when you have problems you can't solve yourself, it is all right to get someone else to help you. Learning to face the problems rather than to run away is an important lesson for them. Everybody wants to avoid pain, and we all try to run away from it in different ways: we drink, use drugs, bury ourselves in work, or take up hobbies or sports that become all-consuming interests; we allow television to become a drug for all our waking hours; we sleep, overeat, retreat into silence—anything to avoid facing a painful situation. To pursue pleasure and avoid pain is the mark of our society.

For this reason many people go on for years in marriages that are destructive to the adults and the children, refusing to do anything about the relationship, either to improve it or end it. This kind of situation is destructive to children. We may be reflecting the kind of relationship we experienced in the family in which we grew up. We learn first about marriage by observing the marriage of our parents. We learn about parenting by being parented.

Now that you and your spouse have finally decided that the time has come to do something about your relationship, it is appropriate for you to tell the children. Where, when, how, what, and who are the questions. It is time for you to take seriously the responsibility for teaching your children some of the most important lessons they will ever learn: how to face and deal with adversity, how to handle stress, how to make claims for yourself without disregarding the needs of others, and how to be courageous.

Take your time to think things through before you tell the children. We saw a couple a few years ago, Bob and Mary, who told us about their impetuousness:

We had been fighting the whole weekend. When Sunday night came, we had both had all we could take. We were screaming at each other, and both of us were so worn out and disgusted with ourselves that we weren't thinking straight anymore.

Finally (Bob said), I told Mary that we might as well get a divorce, and I slammed out of the house and went to see a good friend of mine who is a lawyer. I told him that I wanted him to start divorce proceedings Monday morning. I don't know if he believed me, but when I came back to the house I told Mary what I had done and she blew up and wanted to wake up the kids and tell them.

At first I agreed with her. Then, thank goodness, she decided that we should wait. We had a good night's sleep, and the next morning we were able to think much more clearly. That's when we decided to get help, and I'm so grateful that we didn't rush into telling the kids.

After both of you have had time to consider carefully what you are doing, then ideally, both of you should be involved in deciding how to go about telling the children. We're aware that this is not always possible, especially when one of the parents is not available, either by design or geography. But it helps the children if the parents can at least agree on the manner and content of telling them what is happening.

When to Tell the Children

Let's suppose that you have been involved in counseling. Ideally, you will have told the children something about the progress. They may have been involved in the counseling sessions and so they are aware that you are working on problems. If they are not involved at all or only in some of the sessions, they probably will be curious about how you are getting along. In that case it's a good thing to describe some of the procedure, such as: "We are trying to learn how to communicate better," or "We are trying to learn more about the families in which we grew up." What you say depends on the ages of the children and their capacity for understanding what you mean. It may be good to let them know that some of the problems are very difficult to solve and you don't know if they can be solved satisfactorily. If you then decide to end the marriage, the children will have had some warning.

They should be told just as soon as both of you agree that you are going to separate. There is nothing more painful than waiting for the inevitable pain to occur. It's like having the dentist hold the drill over your head while he tells you a long story. When you are sure, tell the children. If you don't agree, but one of you is determined to leave, then the person leaving may have to do the telling.

Some couples feel that it is better for the children to have time to adjust to the idea before the parent actually leaves, in much the same way that a long illness sometimes provides the family with time for grieving before a death.

On the other hand, a long time between announcement and departure may increase the child's hope that the parent will not leave and will perhaps prolong the child's denial of what is going to happen.

In any case it is better for the children to have at least a little time to adjust, rather than being faced with a parent who is about to go out the door with packed bags. Such a confrontation produces the same kind of shock one must face in losing a loved one in sudden death, and the pain is excruciating. When this kind of separation occurs, it is usually because the parent wants to avoid seeing the pain of the children or the spouse, and so he or she elects to depart "cold turkey." To do so is certainly not in the best interest of the child, and it says a great deal about the guilt, shame, and even cowardice of the parent.

There is no perfect time to tell children—they all have different capacities for adjustment—but probably there is a middle ground somewhere between a long time before separation and the last minute before the parent leaves. A few weeks before the actual departure and after the clear decision has been made is probably best. This gives the family time to work through the questions that arise—who will live where, when and how often visitation will take place—and will allow the parents time to reassure the children that they are loved and will be the chief concern of their parents. It gives both the children and the adults time to work through some of their pain.

Some couples have so much difficulty in deciding what to do about their marriage that they put the children through what could be called cruel and unusual punishment. Read the situation described by one of our clients whom we will call Donna:

I simply couldn't decide what to do. Chuck had been involved with another woman for over a year. I knew it and so did the children. Our kids are pretty well grown up, and they were fully aware of what was going on. They were angry with both of us. They were embarrassed by their father's affair (and so were the other woman's children) and disgusted with me because I wouldn't throw him out. I made the mistake of giving them blow-by-blow accounts of what he was doing, and every day that the situation continued, the angrier they became. I kept thinking that if I held on a little longer he would come to his senses. He wasn't ready to leave, mainly because he felt guilty and needed time to accumulate money so he could afford to maintain a separate residence.

They avoided him, never gave him a chance to talk about his side, and he never did sit down and tell them what he was feeling or give them some idea of what was going to happen. Their sympathy was all with me, and I have to admit that part of the problem was my fault. We should have talked with the kids about how we got to that point, but we didn't.

In a way, Chuck and Donna were allowing the children to make the decision for them. They tried and convicted their father without a full hearing, and both they and their parents were at fault. The decision to separate is not a decision for children to make. Donna's inability to hold her husband accountable for his actions was her problem, and she was the one to solve it. If she had been willing to force some action, to work on the marriage or end it, the children would have been relieved of much unnecessary pain.

Should Young Children Be Told?

If a child is old enough to understand the words, she or he is old enough to be told that a parent is leaving. Obviously some children can use and comprehend language earlier than others.

This individual development varies so much that it is impossible to set a definite age limit below which one would not tell the child. You certainly would not attempt to discuss this or any serious matter with an infant, but you might with a toddler. How you tell children at the various ages is more important than the age at which you tell them. For example, a three-year-old might be told by her mother, "I won't be living here anymore, but I will see you very often and we can still have a lot of fun together," and then answer any questions that the child may have. An older child might be told, "You know that Daddy and I have been having a lot of trouble getting along. We don't love each other anymore, and we have decided that it is better for all of us if we separate." Older children will comprehend much more and ask more complex questions. Other than the very young child, all of them are entitled to know what is happening when one of the most important persons in their lives is about to leave.

Who Should Do the Telling

We believe it is better that both parents are present when the children are told about the plans for a separation. If one of the parents is opposed to the separation, it may be difficult for him or her to face the children without a great deal of emotion. The other parent may fear facing the children because of the likelihood of being seen as "the bad guy." When making plans to tell the children, both parents need to ask themselves what is the best thing for the children and to have the courage to carry it through. Certainly, if both parents are present, it is more supportive than having just one. It sets the example for their facing the many hard decisions that have to be made in the coming months, and it lets the children know that they can talk about the most difficult matters with both their parents.

While it would be inadvisable to talk to the children at a time when either or both parents are overwhelmed by their feelings, allowing the children to see that you hurt is not a bad thing. In fact, it helps them to know that this experience is painful for you, just as it is for them. If you talk about separation and divorce without any sign of emotion or pain, they will certainly wonder why it is so hurtful to them and perhaps will hold back their feelings as a way of protecting you. This protective stance can have some long-term detrimental effects on the child.

Telling the children separately raises the possibility that one of the partners will tell the children that the other partner is the one causing all the problems, and the children will come to believe that one person is innocent and the other one is guilty. People who can be adult in their outlook and healthy in their responses should be able to admit that both parties have contributed to the situation. Hearing about the separation with both parents present provides the opportunity for both persons to be heard. If they can put aside their bitter feelings, they may be able to let the children know that there is responsibility on both sides.

If parents cannot be together without lashing out at each other and causing an even more painful situation, then the next alternative would be to have each parent talk with the children alone. While this is not the ideal, it certainly is better than their hearing only one side, though the danger is that the parents will give very different reasons for the problems, thus confusing the children.

The children should be the first to know when the decision has been made. The danger is that if others know before the children are told, there is a chance that someone other than the parents will be the one who reveals the information to them. Being informed by someone else is very hard for children to accept, and they are rightfully angry with parents who have given this vital information to someone else before they were told. Marilyn told us what happened to her:

I didn't really know what to say to the kids. Hal came home one night and announced he was leaving. He had waited till the kids were in bed. He packed a couple of suitcases and walked out. I was a basket case, not knowing where to turn. My mother came over to stay with the kids the next day while I was at work. She was very supportive and would never have done anything deliberately to upset the children. But while they were having a nap, she thought, she decided to call her sister and tell her what had happened. The kids overheard and Billy, the five-year-old, got hysterical.

"You lied to me," he screamed when I got home. "You told me Daddy had to go out of town, and Nana said he was going to get a divorce. You lied; you lied! You told Nana and you didn't tell me the truth."

Marilyn hadn't intended to lie to the children, but she had not yet decided how and what to tell them. Her husband, Hal, had left without any apparent thought about what might happen with the kids.

What and How Much to Tell

Tell them the truth. The question of whether you tell them all of the details is something you should decide between you. If one of the parents is involved in an extra-marital affair, the "innocent" party may feel that the children deserve to know. If we could have an ideal situation, we would opt to have the couple work out their decision ahead of time about how much to tell the children and the way to tell them. This position is not to say that we are advocating that sometimes you should lie. On the contrary, we feel strongly that whatever you decide to tell the children should be truthful. The issue is rather for you to determine what you feel is your private business and then be prepared to tell the children that there are some things you cannot share with them right now because it is private, but that someday you may decide to do so.

Realistically, we know that in most cases this kind of agreement is hard to reach because there is often too much anger and fear and sadness to allow the two people to reason their way through the situation. We try always to encourage the couple to put aside their own feelings as much as they can and concentrate on the best interests of their children. Blaming each other or trying to get even is not in the best interests of the children. They have to struggle with so much when their family is breaking up that it is grossly unfair to increase their burden by having parents tear each other limb from limb in the presence of their children.

Saying to young children, "Mommy doesn't love Daddy anymore, and she has decided to live with someone else," would be much better than, "Mommy has been cheating on Daddy, and he has decided that she can't live here anymore." Even better would be, "We are not happy together anymore. Something went wrong with our marriage, and we haven't been able to work it out; so we have decided that we won't live together, but we will always be your parents and love you and take care of you."

Older children can understand more. You might be able to let them know more detail. "I fell in love with someone else" is a simple statement of fact. You might, of course, preface that statement with an explanation that you haven't been happy for a long time, that there seemed to be no way that the marriage could be saved, and that without setting out to do so, you found someone else.

It would help if you had decided, before confronting the children, what the details of the separation are going to be. For instance, it would help if you could say that the partner who is leaving is going to live in an apartment nearby or that the children are going to live with whomever you have decided. Remember that their first thought is apt to be "What's going to happen to me?"

Small children should be told where they are going to live and not be given a choice in the matter. It is too difficult for them. With older children, you can give them a choice so long as you make it clear that neither of you will mind which way it goes. Perhaps you can talk with them about what would be most convenient, where they feel they would be most comfortable, and so forth. Keep the discussion on the "best arrangement," not on which parent the child prefers. Before you enter this discussion you had better be sure you won't be devastated if the child chooses the other parent. Otherwise, don't get involved in choices at all. You can emphasize that wherever the child lives the other parent will want to spend a lot of time with him or her, and that you both are in favor of doing so.

There are many things that small children can't understand and should not be expected to understand. So don't tell them more than they need to know. One has to be reminded of the old story about the father whose son came to him and asked, "Where did I come from?" The father with much trepidation launched into the whole subject of sex. At the end of the long explanation, the father asked, "Now, Johnny, why did you ask?" "Oh," said Johnny, "Billy told me he comes from Pittsburgh, and I just wondered where I came from." It might be well to think in terms of telling the children the facts of what is happening and what the separation means to the life of the family in terms of change. Then give the children an opportunity to ask questions to which you can respond. By being as clear and as truthful as you can at this important time in their lives, you may be able to establish a pattern of openness and honesty that will encourage the children to come back to you, feeling free to ask whatever questions are on their minds from time to time.

When we talk about keeping emotions under control, we are not suggesting that you can or should hide the fact that you have some deep feelings about what is happening. There's nothing wrong with all of you having a good cry together. A reasonable time of sharing grief with your children can draw you closer to them. And there's nothing wrong with saying that you feel angry or hurt or sad about the situation. But that is different from saying, "Your mother is a no-good cheating so and so."

Be realistic about telling the children. If you and your spouse cannot treat each other with some kind of dignity, if you cannot hold yourselves together enough to have this kind of session with the children without fighting, then don't do it together. Each of you has the responsibility for what has happened; if you can be adult and accept what you did, then you can avoid the possibility of hurting your children more than they will be anyhow.

Blaming and attacking each other forces the children either to withdraw—run away—or to take sides. While you may deep down wish that they would take your side, they do so at great cost. They love both their parents and should be able to express that love without having to risk hurting the other parent.

The whole matter of assessing blame is a complicated one. In their attempts to understand what has happened, children often will blame themselves—"If I had been a better boy . . .," "If only I had helped Mommy more . . .," "If we kids didn't argue so much. . . ." Thus they may go on "what-iffing" their way toward trying to make sense of this difficult situation. Even if they do not raise the issue, you need to reassure them over and over that only the two adults are responsible for what has happened, that the children did not cause the problem, nor could they have prevented it. Do not assume that having told them once, the worry is over. They can sometimes get physically or emotionally ill from worrying about their part in this problem.

Jamie was a dear little eight-year-old when we saw him. He was so depressed that his mother was fearful that he would harm himself.

> I noticed that he kept taking off his seatbelt in the car, and we never allow that. When I scolded and scolded, and still he did it, I finally realized that he was hoping he would get hurt. I can't imagine why he would do such a thing because he is so important to all of us.

Jamie finally revealed to us that before his father left, he had been very angry at Jamie for using some tools that he wasn't supposed to touch, and Jamie had connected the leaving with his own behavior. Fortunately, the father was willing to take part in the child's therapy, and the boy finally accepted the fact that his father had planned to leave long before the incident with the tools.

Children need reassurance on another issue. The parent who has custody needs to reassure the children constantly that he or she is not going to leave also. They may think, "If one of my parents can leave me, what is to prevent the other one from leaving?" Very young children may panic when the remaining parent goes out for an evening or even leaves the child to go on errands. Their trust has been broken, and they are not sure what they can believe anymore. Thus, the very difficult task of rebuilding trust must be undertaken, painful though it may be.

When one parent has disappeared, the custodial parent may make attempts to assure the children that their other parent still loves them. Marguerite told us:

> I don't know what to say to my little girl. She was very young when her father left, and she hasn't seen him for several years, not even a phone call or a letter or card. I can't believe he could be so cruel, but I keep on telling Jennifer that he does love her and he will come back

someday. She's reached the point where she doesn't believe me anymore.

How could she believe that someone loves her who has abandoned her, who never cares to contact her? Jennifer is being more realistic than her mother, and the problem is that now she doesn't believe that her mother will tell her the truth. Marguerite had the best of intentions. She wanted Jennifer to feel secure in the knowledge that her father loved her and perhaps Marguerite was sincere in her belief or hope that he would someday come back. But it is not fair for her to attempt to interpret the father's feelings. She might better have let Jennifer know that she understood the pain Jennifer was feeling and that she herself was frustrated in not knowing where the father was or what he intended to do.

Children will sometimes attempt to make decisions for their parents. They will do everything they can to try to reverse decisions about separation. One father told us:

> Our boys were determined that we weren't going to separate. They reminded us of all the things we had told them about settling disagreements. "You can work it out," they said. "You told us that when you have a fight with someone you have to negotiate. You said that both sides should give in a little, and then you could work out your problems. How come you two don't do that?" They cried, they screamed at us, they were very, very angry that we wouldn't listen to their pleas. We had worked very hard at trying to save the marriage, and it had reached the point where we both knew it was over. Fortunately, we had gone through this process before we told the boys. When they saw that we really meant it, we were surprised how quickly they began to turn to the questions of just exactly what was going to happen to them. They didn't give up without a fight, but I think we helped them by being able to stand firm and not allow them to make our decisions. We did admit to them that we had been wrong in not preparing them for the fact that there were problems that could not be solved.

Sometimes grown-up children are put in a difficult position by their parents' marital problems. We know of a very prominent family where the husband had been having an affair for years. Everyone knew about it, including the wife. Their three children found it more and more difficult to visit the parents because they felt sorry for the mother, and angry with their father. Both parents pretended that everything was fine while the children visited, but there was so much tension in the family that it became unbearable. These grown-up children finally decided that they had to do something. They realized that it was inappropriate for them to tell their parents *what* to do about their marriage, but they felt entitled to have them come to terms with the situation and either work on the marriage or end it. They decided to face their parents, not accusing one and defending the other (they were wise enough to know there was fault on both sides), but to confront the problem and ask their parents to do something about it.

> We told them we loved them both and that we were not going to tell them what they should do, but that we wanted them to know the pain they were inflicting on the whole family as well as themselves and that the time had come for them to face their problems. We even told them we didn't want to see them until they had made a decision.
>
> It took a long time for them to come to terms. Our father left for a while and then finally realized what he was giving up. They are back together now, and they have never been happier. Dad has given up his affair, and it looks as if they are really working on their marriage.

This is a case of the children parenting their parents; their action was decisive in ending a very difficult and painful situation. Still, they did not try to force divorce or reconciliation, but they stated their own position—that of loving children whose parents were hurting, and in turn, hurting them.

What should the parents tell the children? In short, tell them as much of the truth as they are old enough to handle; tell them you love them and will never abandon them; tell them how you feel and encourage them to share their feelings with you. They will make it if you do.

Telling the School

As soon as you have made up your minds to separate, it is very important that you share this information with other persons who are playing a significant role in your child's life. In addition to members of the extended family, the school needs to know. Your child spends a lot of his or her waking hours in school, and the teacher and the guidance counselor can be very helpful if they know that your child is going through a difficult time. These school people really want to be of help, but it is up to you to let them know how to help. Just as you would share the information about a death in the family, you need to be brave about facing the teacher or other appropriate school personnel. Not very many children are willing to share this information voluntarily. Many of them, in fact, are not willing to accept the reality of the situation and will pretend that the parent is not going to leave, or that he or she is coming back soon. Some children are ashamed of what is happening in the family, and they are thus reluctant to have anyone know.

This time creates tremendous stress for the children, whether they are in elementary, junior, or senior high school. If the teacher is aware of the children's needs, it may be possible to build in some stress-relieving activities during the school day. Elementary school teachers can pair your child with others who have been through a divorce and can share with your child how they handled the situation.

If the family is going to have to move, let the school know as soon as possible so that the teachers can try to bring some closure on the children's lives in the school. They may be able to have the class talk about changes that happen in families and how it feels.

Many schools, aware of the growing number of students who have to visit noncustodial parents on weekends, are deciding not to make assignments over weekends, but confine them to the rest of the week. Other schools are establishing support groups for children, particularly at the secondary level, though even young children can benefit from this kind of group.

After you have a custody agreement, take it to the school and let them be aware of what is and what is not permitted as far as their sharing school records with the noncustodial parent. Schools are willing to hold separate conferences with the noncustodial parents if the agreement permits it. We strongly recommend that the noncustodial parent be allowed to have some part in the child's school life, unless, of course, he or she is using the school performance as a weapon over the head of the custodial parent—for example, attempting to show that the custodial parent is not doing a good job and therefore should not be allowed to maintain custody.

There are many persons on the staff of the school who can be helpful to you at this time—the school social worker, the school psychologist, or nurse. You should know that in some schools the number of children from single-parent homes exceeds half the school population. Many school professionals are very knowledgeable and can be a great resource for you.

If it is difficult for you to find the time to go to the school, send a note to the teacher explaining what is happening. This need not contain all the gory details. Simply state the facts and call on the teacher or guidance counselor to be sensitive to your child's school behavior. You should expect that this information will be handled with discretion and that you and the school can work together with the purpose of helping your child through this very difficult time.

The same process should be followed, of course, with the church school and any other significant persons—music teacher, coach, youth advisers, pastor, and others.

3

Decisions, Decisions

With a faraway look in her eyes, Dorothy gave a long sigh and reflected on the year following her decision to seek a divorce:

In the beginning I thought that the hardest decision we had to make was what to do about our marriage. As I look back now, that was easy. The hardest thing was what to do about the kids. We made such a mess of it—fighting over the kids as if they were property—that I wonder if they will ever be able to forgive us.

Married for twenty-two years, Dorothy and Ned had four children. Their eldest, Brian, had long ago given up on the family and was out on his own living with a young woman. He seldom saw the family. Marjorie (sixteen), Emily (fourteen), and Billy (nine) were at home. The custody battle had ended with Marjorie and Billy living with their mother, and Emily with her father. Unable to settle the matter themselves, a court had made the decision for them. As is usual in such cases, the judge had conferred with the older children and had acceded to their wishes. Emily worried about her father living alone and thus had expressed a wish to live with him. In spite of the fact that Dorothy had promised the children that they should feel free to make their own decisions, she felt hurt and angry when Emily chose to live with her father. Marjorie and Billy felt that Emily was abandoning them, and they made life miserable for Emily when she came to visit her mother.

Emily reached the point where she didn't want to come to the house at all, and the other kids refused to visit their father. It was only then that I came to my senses and decided that we had to stop fighting over our children and act like adults. How I wish we had been able to put aside our selfishness and make it easier for our children.

There is no easy way to decide what to do about the children of divorce. Whichever way a custody decision is made, it will hurt someone. Even the most irresponsible parent hurts deeply when separated from his or her children. Something deep within each of us causes us to long for connection with our offspring. With responsible, loving parents the pain is more obvious, the wound more severe. The same is true of children. All children want to be with their parents, would prefer to have their parents together, even in cases of abuse. And all children benefit from having two parents. As one writer puts it, we can get along with one kidney or one ear, and we can get along with one eye. But having two eyes gives us a wider field of vision, better depth perception. If it is not possible to have two parents in the home, then the next best thing is to make certain that the children have access to both parents as often as possible. Many custody decisions are being made these days on the basis of which parent is most likely to give adequate care *and which parent is most likely to allow free access to the other parent.*

One of the givens about custody is that the decision reached at the beginning of the separation process is often not the final one. Couples find that their circumstances change; they find that the parent awarded custody of a particular child may not be able to handle him or her; the noncustodial parent may decide to fight the battle to obtain custody over and over again. Through it all, the children may feel that they are being bounced back and forth like a football. They may become bitter about the fact that so much money is being spent by their warring parents while they are deprived of financial support for their basic needs, to say nothing of losing resources that might be applied to their education.

What Are the Options for Custody?

There are basically three kinds of custody arrangements: (1) *sole or exclusive custody*, which means that one parent cares for the children on a daily basis, takes responsibility for the children's needs and for decisions that have to be made regarding them, such as basic needs, health, schooling, and discipline; (2) *split custody,* which means that the children are split between the two parents, with each parent taking sole responsibility for the child or children in his or her care; and (3) *joint custody*, which means that both parents can share in the decisions and responsibilities for the children. Joint custody doesn't always mean that the sharing is equal, and the arrangement can be as flexible as the parents wish it to be. It usually does mean that the parents live in the same area so that the children can continue to attend the same school and stay in contact with friends and with their normal activity schedules. Joint custody works best when the parents are on very good terms with each other and are willing to put aside their battles and concentrate on making the move back and forth between the parents as easy as possible for the children. The custody arrangements in this case vary widely. Some parents share the children on a part-week basis, some every other week, and some every other month. Some plan for the children to be with one parent for the winter and with the other parent for the summer and holidays. We heard of one couple who worked out an arrangement where the children stayed in the family home and the parents moved in and out. Another couple who left the children in the home worked different shifts, and they arranged to have one parent home days and the other nights.

Judges across the country are becoming more open to the possibility of awarding custody to fathers, but in most cases they are much more apt to award custody to the mother except in special circumstances. In spite of the fact that the majority of all mothers are working outside the home, they are still largely responsible for the rearing of children. They are the "psychological" parent in most cases, making most of the decisions regarding discipline, meal preparation, choice of clothing, care during illness, and so on. Where this is not the case, if the father is equally responsible for family decisions and operation of the household, or if the mother is deemed to be "unfit" (by reason of neglect of children, abuse of drugs or alcohol, or is mentally or physically incompetent), the courts are more willing to consider the father as the sole custodial parent. Many judges are more enlightened than they have been portrayed to be in the past and are depending on the advice of social workers, psychologists, and other professionals who work with the courts. They often do talk with the children, usually in private chambers away from the parents, and with each child separately.

You cannot depend on having such an enlightened judge assigned to your case. Unfortunately there are still many judges in this country who show little concern for the best interests of the child and who exhibit prejudices in favor of one sex over the other as the best custodial parent, or who are susceptible to political influences in their decision making. We hope that the number of such judges is declining, but because of the uncertainty of the process, you are much safer to make the decision outside the judicial process and simply take the agreement to the court for certification. In most cases, unless the judge has strong and compelling reasons for rejecting the arrangement, it will be accepted. You and your spouse, with the help of a divorce mediator, a family counselor, your pastor or other professional, can draw up an agreement, take it to your attorney to have it written in the proper form, and then submit it to the court for ratification.

In 1970 the state of Michigan set up criteria for determining the "best interest of the child," and it seems to us to represent a model for the child-custody process. These criteria were:

1. The love, affection, and other emotional ties existing between the competing parties and the child.
2. The capacity and disposition of competing parties to give the child love, affection, and guidance and continuation of the educating and raising of the child in its religion or creed, if any.
3. The capacity and disposition of competing parties to provide the child with food, clothing, medical care or other remedial care recognized and permitted under the laws

of this state in lieu of medical care, and other material needs.

4. The length of time the child has lived in a stable, satisfactory environment and the desirability of maintaining continuity.
5. The permanence, as a family unit, of the existing or proposed custodial home.
6. The moral fitness of the competing parties.
7. The mental and physical health of the competing parties.
8. The home, school, and community record of the child.
9. The reasonable preference of the child, if the court deems the child to be of sufficient age to express preference.
10. Any other factor considered by the court to be relevant to a particular child custody dispute.

Formal vs. Informal Custody Arrangements

We believe strongly in having a legal custody agreement, rather than simply an informal understanding between the parents. However well-meaning you are, no matter how much you trust each other now, circumstances can change and the battle may begin all over again. Children benefit from knowing that there is a legal agreement. They sometimes will threaten to go live with the other parent if the custodial parent makes rules they don't agree with, or if they have found that they can exploit the parent by such threats. A noncustodial parent may be filled with guilt about having relinquished custody to the spouse and may try to relieve the guilt by subtly luring the child away from the custodial parent. Having the legal right to custody, the parent is in a much better position to tell the child firmly that he or she has no choice but must stay with the custodial parent.

On the other hand, having such an agreement does not mean it can never be changed. As you work through the process, you may decide to ask the court to make changes. If both parents are willing, this will be very easy to do.

Visitation Rights

We believe strongly that children are entitled to have access to both their parents. This is true even in cases where there has been neglect or abuse of the child. The safety of the child can be assured by permitting visitation only with a third party present and in controlled circumstances. Of course there may be rare instances where the child's physical or emotional health is at risk, and in those cases it would be foolish to expose the child to the risk involved in visitation, but those cases are unusual.

In our experience, the freer the children are to visit back and forth between their parents, the better they adjust to the divorce. Open visitation requires cooperation between the parents and excellent communication. If this flexibility cannot be achieved, or if one of the parents is irresponsible in carrying out the arrangement, then a more structured one would be preferable. In the beginning of separation, many couples feel that it is better if the noncustodial parent comes to the house to visit the children (especially where the children are young), and the custodial parent arranges to go away from home during those times. This approach sometimes has its disadvantages since the children may have to deal with their feelings of abandonment every time the parent leaves. It may also prolong the agony of disengagement for the parents, and it may be a subtle way of hanging on by a spouse who refuses to let go of the marriage. With this arrangement the custodial parent also may find it very difficult to begin a new social life if he or she is never sure when the noncustodial parent may visit.

If parents can agree on basic values and discipline for their children, then the visitation can be carried on in a way that gives the children a consistent and trustable pattern for their lives. We recognize that this consistency may not be possible, since a difference in values may have been the reason for the divorce. But responsible parents can be sure that if they refuse to get into a tug-of-war over the children, if they maintain the standards they believe in, the children in the long run will benefit from their courage.

What Is the Best Custody Arrangement for My Child?

In her book *The Complete Book of Child Custody,* Suzanne Ramos sets forth some excellent questions for parents who are considering what custody arrangement is best for them.

If You're Thinking About One-Parent Custody:
1. Do you believe that you are the "psychological parent" of

your children? (Experts at the Yale Child Study Center now say that in almost every family, there is clearly one parent who is the psychological parent.)

2. Are you and your spouse bitter toward one another or not on cooperative terms? (If so, joint custody would be unwise.)

3. Do you like having children around, not just your own, but their friends too? Do you mind feeding them and cleaning up after them?

4. Do you have the patience and the determination to discipline and train children so that they have a sense of order in their lives and so that they:

a. learn to do things for themselves (bathe, brush their teeth, take care of their clothes, do their homework, practice the piano, handle money);

b. learn acceptable, polite behavior and can handle themselves in social situations; and,

c. learn to be considerate of and helpful to you, to each other, and to others? These may sound like simple tasks but they require years of perseverance on your part.

5. Can you remove splinters, treat wounds, pull loose teeth, give tepid baths when fevers run high, give shampoos?

6. More importantly, can you handle emotional wounds or problems? Do your children find you sensitive to their feelings and, therefore, trust you and confide in you? Essentially, do you connect with them emotionally?

7. Can you allow them a certain amount of childish behavior—crying, being jealous of a sister or brother, bad dreams, anxiety—without becoming angry?

8. Are you affectionate and physical with your children?

9. Can you cook—fix breakfasts during the morning rush, pack lunches, and prepare nutritious meals offering more variety than hamburgers and spaghetti?

10. Are you willing to handle housework—laundry, marketing, cleaning kitchens and bathrooms, vacuuming, picking up after the children, sewing torn seams, replacing buttons, ironing a shirt or dress for a special occasion—and give up the eight to ten hours a week necessary to take care of these things?

11. If you work full-time, can you be home for a reasonable amount of time during the week when the children are home? For example, can you be with them for dinner on at least three out of five weekday evenings?

12. Do you have, or know where to find, someone reliable, kind and intelligent to be there when the children come home from school, someone who can stay if you have to work late?

13. Can you take time off from work if one of your children is sick, has a day off, or is on vacation from school? If not, do you have a good substitute?

14. Can you attend a fair number of PTA meetings and parent-

teacher conferences? Can you get away for some daytime school events, such as class plays, field days, and the like? Will you volunteer occasionally for some of the many jobs parents are called upon to do to help make the school run smoothly?

15. Can you drop everything and leave work if the school calls and says your child has a temperature or just vomited in the classroom?

16. Are you willing to try and cope with a child saying to you, "If my parents hadn't gotten a divorce, maybe I would do better in school" ("maybe I would be happier") ("maybe I wouldn't be overweight") . . . ?

17. How do you feel about having your personal life secondary to your parental responsibilities: being able to meet fewer people socially; at times, having to cancel plans at the last minute because one of your children is sick or the baby-sitter can't make it; having a limited sex life?

18. Do you know that you will probably feel that you never have *enough* money, quiet, adult conversation, sex, *time*—time to be with your children, to concentrate on your work, to keep the house in order, to get out with friends?

19. Do you know that, in spite of all your work, you probably won't get much appreciation?

20. Do you feel that your children are special and irresistible? That having them with you will make all the sacrifices worthwhile?

21. Are you willing to take on whatever emotional problems your children may have in reaction to the separation, at a time when you, yourself, may not be feeling too strong?

22. Do you feel that you should assume exclusive custody because you are the more loving, more responsible, better parent?

23. Have you asked your children what living arrangement they would like? This is essential where children are approximately ten or older. Even younger children should be consulted, although their opinions should not be controlling.

If You're Thinking About Joint Custody:

1. Do you sincerely believe that both of you have an equally close emotional bond with your children? That you share the role of "psychological parent" and are not depriving them of being with the one parent who really is the closer to the children—the one they talk to, trust, love, and depend on more than the other? (Parents often report having overheard their children ask each other, "Who do you like better, Mommy or Daddy?" with the children giving thoughtful but very definite answers.) Many others feel that one parent should almost always be given the dominant role, because joint custody, with its dual living arrangements, puts too great a strain on children. It is often too disruptive for young children and frequently doesn't last long with teenagers,

who generally want to live in one place—where their friends and social lives are, where they can bring friends, and where they have a calm, stable life during what are difficult years.

2. Do neither of you want full-time custody?

3. Do both of you work outside the home?

4. Do you have a good working relationship with your former spouse?

5. Are you prepared to talk to him/her as often as every day to discuss your mutual responsibilities regarding the children—school, health care, discipline, extracurricular activities, dates with friends?

6. Do you live within a few miles of your former spouse?

7. Are you prepared for the inconvenience of your child moving in and out every few days, every week, or every month?

8. Can you handle all of the responsibilities mentioned under one-parent custody? While you will not have the children full time, you will have them enough of the time so that you will have to provide full parental services—physical, emotional, intellectual, social. If your children are with you for roughly 50 percent of the time, that time with you is part of their real life and should not have the off-schedule tone that is often the case when children "visit" a noncustodial parent for a day or weekend.

9. What living arrangement do your children say they would like?

If You're Thinking About Split Custody:

1. How will your children feel about being separated from one another and how difficult will it be for them? Remember, children lend each other support and they can be especially helpful to each other following a separation.

2. Have you thought about how many other adjustments this will involve for your child at the same time [she/he] must cope with your divorce? Will [she/he] have to:

a. move to a new home? a new part of the country?

b. change schools?

c. give up most friends?

d. learn a new language?

3. Have you explored other, less drastic arrangements and found them unworkable (such as split/joint custody—see 9.)?

4. Have you thought about the recommendations on split custody of some psychiatrists who say that:

a. If there are three children in your family, you might consider separating the middle, sometimes more neglected, child and leave the oldest and youngest together;

b. where there is an older boy and a younger girl, the boy might go with the father and the girl with the mother?

5. Are your children more than six years apart in age? (This would probably make the separation easier on them.)

6. Are you and your former spouse going to be separated by a great distance? If the distance between you would prohibit anything more than one trip a year, this strengthens the argument for split custody—provided the children are not very close.

7. Do you realize that children can provide help and support to a custodial parent, thereby improving the home atmosphere for all? Older children often help with and act as surrogate parents to younger children. Breaking up the children precludes this support system.

8. Do you in any way think of your children as possessions? Could it be that, without realizing it, you feel that having custody of none of the children would be "giving" too much to your spouse, and for that reason, you want split custody?*

Sorting out the right questions to ask is half the battle. We certainly would not suggest that a person has to hammer out answers to all the questions about joint custody and one-parent custody before making a move. People can drown in a sea of questions. A labyrinth of questions can entice one into a dismal floundering without direction. But, with no questions at all, a person can bravely set out travelling a dead-end street.

Sort through the parade of questions listed. Think through the issues that these questions reflect. The discipline will help in finding that kind of focus that gives decision-making power and forward movement.

When the key issues have been opened up, it is a truism that no one can make the decisions for you. There is no way to take the edge off the four-step approach to decision making:

1. Know what the issue is you are trying to solve;
2. Gather all the information you have at hand about it;
3. Listen carefully to the opinions of trusted counselors and friends who have reasons to be knowledgeable through their own experience or their special expertise;
4. Then make your own decision.

How often we hear people say that they decided as they did, and they acted as they did because "they"—meaning some member of the family or friends or a counselor or some other outside person—said it was the right thing to do. Very often people who are insecure feel more comfortable if they can say to themselves that someone else made the decision. This pro-

*Suzanne Ramos, *The Complete Book of Child Custody* (New York: G. P. Putnam's Sons, 1979), pp. 103-110. Reprinted by permission of G. P. Putnam's Sons. Copyright © 1979 by Suzanne Ramos.

vides a false security of not being responsible in case the decision turns out to be ineffective. The old Adam and Eve dodge, "I didn't do it; someone told me to," will not stand up as an excuse.

Relying on others to make decisions for you will not help you. It is not fair to them nor fair to you, for in the long run if you are to grow to your true potential, you will have to find the courage to make decisions for yourself. This, of course, will require you to be willing to take some risks—risking that the decisions you make will be wrong, and then to be willing to take the responsibility for your actions. This is the way one acts in an adult fashion—not always to be looking for someone else to make a decision and to take the blame when things don't turn out well—as a child would. You want to grow and decision making is one way to help you do so.

There was a woman we once knew who was a well-informed, intelligent woman. However, over the years she had the reputation of never hazarding her own opinion on any subject. When questioned, she would look around awaiting a cue from someone else. She relied on her husband to have the opinions about everything: religion, politics, household management, parenting, finances. She even took pride in being what she supposed was supportive of her husband by not intruding with her own opinions. It surprised her one day when her husband talked about terminating the marriage. Genuinely perplexed, she asked, "Why?" Painfully, she learned that he no longer considered her companionable, that he felt she had little or nothing to offer in their relationship. As for parenting, she appeared to him to be a very weak parent. She always deferred to him when it came to matters relating to the behavior of the children.

Fortunately, this woman sought help. She began to see what it really meant to have no opinion, to be unable to claim a decision on her own. She saw how she was moving to an emptiness without attraction to anyone, and without meaning to her family or to herself. She began the slow recovery of the ability to say "I" and to be a whole person.

We apply this insight to the matter of custody agreements. Negotiation, as we have indicated earlier, is required. Negotiation, however, is seldom successful unless the people involved become explicit in what they want. Approaching the negotiation with a cat-and-mouse stance (that is, waiting to see what move provides the occasion for pouncing), guarantees less than satisfaction in the long run. Using the occasion to "get even" or to "show power" or to vent anger likewise diminishes the chances for solutions that can be supportive of the children.

Custody negotiations call for adult behavior on the part of the parents. The success hinges on the ability of the adults to state clearly their perception of the arrangement that offers the greatest support to the children. This level of success, in turn, requires people to have confidence in their own judgments and at the same time to listen seriously and weigh carefully what the other is saying.

A strong supportive custody arrangement can provide security to the child when the parents are open and responsible in the negotiations that lead to that custody decision.

MOTHER

VS

FATHER

4

Children in the Middle

Probably the most difficult issue that children have to handle is the matter of how they can love both parents without being disloyal to either. This is brought home most poignantly when the child describes his or her dilemma. As one ten-year-old told us, out of the hearing distance of either parent:

> I really don't know what to do. I know how upset my mother is about Daddy's leaving us, and I'm mad at him, too, but I really do want to see him. I don't let her know because she would be really hurt and it would make her cry. She keeps telling me it's OK, but I can tell she is very lonely when I leave her. It's almost like she wishes he wouldn't ever come to see me. She wants me to tell him how mad I am with him, but I can't. He would never want to see me again.

This little girl is caught in the middle. She can't move any closer to her father without upsetting her mother. And if she stays close to her mother and keeps her from feeling unhappy, then she may lose what little contact she has with her father now.

How unfair it is to put children in this situation. Of course many parents do it unwittingly. They know it is best for the children to see both parents, and they encourage them to do so, but their actions truly speak loud and clear that they don't want it. Children are like barometers. They don't have to be told because they *feel* the slightest change in their parents.

It took me a long time when our children were little to recognize that their moods often reflected my own. If I was feeling grumpy, they were grumpy. If I was feeling happy and carefree, so were they. We can't fool them by saying one thing and feeling something else. They will know.

It is important for you to do more than simply say you want the children to see their other parent. You must insist on it, must let them know that you have plans for doing things while they are gone, and actually plan for their time away to be your leisure and relaxation time. It can be an important part of maintaining your strength and good mental health. This personal time is an advantage, not a disadvantage. How many married people would welcome a regular opportunity to be free of the responsibilities of child care for a day or two?

Let the children make a claim on their other parent for time with that parent. If you try to force the issue, you may create a big fight over the fact that the other parent seems not to care about the child by absenting himself or herself or by being unreliable. Let the child ask for more time, especially school-age children. Even though you are feeling very angry with your former spouse, try your best to keep your remarks in the area of your feelings, rather than in character assassination. You won't have to tell your children that your former spouse is a bad person if she or he is; the children will make up their own minds.

In the same way, it is not a good idea for you to keep telling your children that although their other parent doesn't come to see them, doesn't remember birthdays, continues to break promises and break their hearts (as well as yours), he or she still loves the children. That would seem to be a very strange kind of love, and you certainly don't want to teach your children this meaning of love. You can reflect their feelings—"It is very hard when you don't hear from Daddy," or "I can imagine how truly hurt you feel when you expect to get a birthday present from Mommy and nothing comes." You can say, "I feel very angry with Daddy that he forgot to come last night," or, "Mommy just doesn't seem to be able to think about anything but her own problems at this time. Let's hope that will change soon."

Children as Message Carriers

We meet many divorced people who are, without intent, using their children as message carriers. Unable to talk with their former spouse without a battle, they resort to having the children talk for them. Asking children to carry messages is one of the most common ways in which parents split the loyalties of their children.

> Tell your father that if he can't pick you up on time, you're not going to go with him next time. I don't care what his excuse is. You can tell him for me that I'm plenty fed up, and I'm not going to let you go!

Now what can the child do? If she delivers the message, her father is going to be angry with her as well as her mother. The child wants to protect her mother, and she doesn't want to risk her father's anger. Still, if she doesn't deliver the message, her mother will be angry. If she doesn't tell him, she will be met at home with the question, "What did he say?" Suppose the father has blown up and made some derogatory remarks about the mother. The child is now in a box, unable to do anything that will solve the problem. The only way out would be for the child to find the courage to tell her parents to deliver their own messages. This is not to say we don't recognize that communication between divorced people is very difficult in many cases. It may be the chief reason why the couple couldn't make a success of the marriage. But it is to say that continuing to use the child to carry the messages is not acceptable.

Faced with the fact that they are exploiting their children, splitting their loyalties, most parents are willing to try harder to keep their lines of communication open. Even if one parent is unwilling to try, the other one can make a difference in this kind of situation by becoming more aware of the child's dilemma and appealing to the former spouse to find a way to work out the details of visitation without involving the children. If this is not possible, then the concerned parent will have to force a change, either through the help of a third party (some kind of counseling) or through the courts, unpleasant as that may be.

Children as Spies

Another way that children get caught between their parents is when they are asked to report on their parents' activities or on relationships. "Was his girl friend there? What did you do with her? Is she living there with him? Were they lovey-dovey?" "Did Mommy go out with that guy again? Did she take you to his house?"

It simply is not fair to ask your child to spy on his or her parent and report back to you. What is to be accomplished by it? We have seen children so upset by having to go through this kind of questioning that they become very fearful of moving back and forth between their parents. Although they long for a relationship with the absent parent, they will make all kinds of excuses, even become physically ill, rather than to have to report to either parent about the other. Or, conversely, some children catch onto this dynamic and try to use it as leverage on the parents for their own advantage.

This kind of grilling usually is an indication that the parents have not let go of their former relationship. They are still trying to hold on by keeping tabs on each other. If this is the case, it becomes doubly difficult for the children to get through the transition period themselves. They know that at least one of their parents is still holding on, and in some cases where there is little or no hope for a reconciliation, the pain is increased for them as they ride the roller coaster of emotions up and down, over and over again.

When children come home from a visit with the noncustodial parent, it is quite proper to ask, "Did you have a nice visit with Daddy?" If the child seems to want to talk more about it, let that happen. Active listening* will enable the child to tell you what he or she wants to say without having to deal with questions that invade the privacy of his or her relationship

---

*See *P.E.T. in Action,* by Thomas Gordon (New York: Wyden Books, 1976). There is a description of active listening in Chapter 4, "Becoming a Listening Parent," pp. 55 ff.

with the other parent. "You seem sad. Is anything bothering you?" would be an appropriate question if you feel the child has something on his or her mind. You can open the door for the child to share a problem with you, but then stand back and allow the child to enter a dialogue with you if he or she wishes. You can reflect the child's feelings as you experience them, saying, "That makes you feel . . ." (sad, happy, fearful, etc.). Such observations are a way to open conversation, whereas invasive questions will cut it off.

Children's Threats

Janet had just returned from the hospital, having undergone surgery for a hysterectomy. She was a beautiful young woman in her early thirties, and she was having a difficult time dealing with the fact that she could no longer bear children. Divorced for over a year, she had two boys (ages eight and ten). They had stayed with their father during her hospital stay. On her first day at home, they came home from school, ran to her bedroom, and announced that they had decided they would like to live with their father.

> I was devastated. It wasn't enough that I had to deal with my physical situation. Here they were telling me that the operation had opened the door for them to have such a ball with their father that they would rather go live with him. He had paid very little attention to them when we were together; he was too involved with his business or getting over a hangover. But this was his way of getting even with me for leaving him. The boys had such a good time—they stayed up till all hours, ate whatever they wished, and he took them everywhere they could dream of going, bought them all kinds of extravagant gifts, things I can't afford. So why wouldn't they prefer him?
>
> The last few days have been hellish. Every time I ask them to do something, they threaten me again—"Well, we'll just go live with Daddy. He doesn't make us do that." I would go through fire and flood for these boys, but I can't compete with their father. Maybe it would be better for them to live with him.

Janet sobbed as she spilled out her story to us. These young boys had found a way to hold her hostage. This was not an unusual situation, but a very dangerous one. We helped Janet to see that where the boys lived was not a question for them to decide. She saw that the adult decision, settled by a long and painful court fight should be decisive. As a matter of fact the father didn't want the boys to live in his apartment. It would be very difficult for him because of the nature of his work which required him to be out of town for long periods of time. She needed to be able to tell her sons that she was sure they had a good time with their father and that she was glad for that. She needed then to inform them that their home was going to be with her, whether they wanted it or not, and that she was not going to discuss it any further. Nor was she going to put up with their trying to threaten her every time she had to discipline them. No doubt their announcement to her was their way of testing her to see if she really wanted to have them with her.

The boys' threats in this instance were very much on the order of the threats that all children use to get their way—"I'm going to run away." You don't have to be a single parent to experience that one. There's an answer that works in most cases—just ask the child to specify where she or he is going. In any case, you don't ignore the child who says he or she is going to run away, but neither do you panic. Remember, you are in charge, and then proceed to let the child know, too. Some parents offer to help the child pack. We've never felt that this was a situation in which you want to play games, even if you are a parent, like most of us, who has occasionally wished that our cantankerous child *would* leave for a while! Children are not so unlike their parents in this way. No doubt there are plenty of times when most children would welcome their parents' departure, at least until they were hungry! Tell them that you love them, that you would miss them terribly if they were to leave, and that they are not permitted to go.

Exploitation of Parents

Children learn very early how to exploit their parents who are divorced. Most children, in all kinds of families, have tried that. Breathes there a child who hasn't found the soft places in the parents' armour? The child of divorce listens ever so

carefully to the parent or the well-meaning grandparent saying, "That poor little thing! It's not his fault that he hasn't any
mommy. We'll have to make it up to him." The child reads the
parent who is filled with guilt very easily. In no time at all,
unless the parents are very careful to avoid it, the child finds
ways to exploit the situation. He or she will play on your
sympathy in order to get you to buy things you really can't
afford or don't want the child to have. The child will learn to
get you to relax rules because you feel sorry for him or her:
"Let me stay up just a little while longer. I'm afraid to go to
bed since Daddy's not here." Or the child may say, "Since I
don't have any mommy——." This appeal is tough to handle,
chiefly because children do have genuine fears as a result of
the change in their lives. You have a thin line to walk between
being exploited and dealing sensitively with the child's real
needs.

You must do all that you can to allay the fears a child has,
and then ask yourself if you are being exploited. One of the
ways you can best help your child to feel secure is to convey
to him or her the assurance that you are in charge and are not
wavering in how you go about making decisions. Of course it's
hard to be prepared to make a decision about serious matters
or even simple ones when you are trying to cope with much
more than ever before. You can decide to relax a rule but temper
that decision with the statement, "I'm going to let you do this
for one time only, and then I will have to consider it more
carefully for any other time." This limitation will give you a
little leeway to think about it overnight or for a few days. If
you are still unsure, ask someone else to help you think it
through.

All parents are faced with uncertainties about their parenting. We all feel we could have done a better job if we had
another chance. Unfortunately we don't have that option, and
we have to learn to live with the mistakes we make. It helps
to know that all parents make mistakes and usually their
children survive.

Your decisions are not chiseled in stone. If you later decide
that you made a mistake, simply say to the child, "I have been
thinking about what I decided the other night, and I don't like
that decision. It was not the best way. Here is what we are

going to do." They may accuse you of going back on your word, but you can say, "No, I didn't give you my promise. I gave you a decision, which I have now decided to change."

The older the child, the more likely you will be faced with more sophisticated exploitation. Teenagers are certainly talented in this field. Of course they need special understanding, and of course they are going through difficult times, but that is all the more reason for you to be determined to keep the quality of family life as close to normal as possible. Young people need structure for their lives; that is, they need to know the limits and they benefit from having a parent with strength to follow through with those limits.

In the case of a home where there has been a great deal of strife and unhappiness, the fact that the turmoil is over should make it more possible to deny the child the license to run away from problems. Running away is what most teenagers will do if they can find a way to make their parent feel sorry for them. Taunts from a teenager, such as "I'm not a kid anymore; you can't tell me what to do," should be met with determination on the part of that child's parent to demonstrate clearly that the parent is in charge and that there will be no permission to disobey the rules.

Children, both young and old, learn to play one parent against the other. They remind one parent that the other one "always takes me to . . . ," or "told me I didn't have to. . . ." Then the parent can easily get trapped in a one-upmanship game. In addition to bankrupting the parent, the children will suffer also, because they are learning how easy it is to manipulate people who love them. Manipulation is a dangerous game because once it has been started, the problems caused can begin to snowball. Instead of allowing yourself to get pulled into the game, be prepared to say something like this: "Well, that's the way it is when you are there, but in this house we will do it this way."

We wouldn't want to indicate that there is no room for compromise in your stance. Especially when the children are older, you may be able to listen carefully to a young person's pleas for change, and sometimes you will find that it is time for you to begin letting go a little. If the young person has demonstrated to you that he or she is capable of responsible behavior, it wouldn't be so terrible if the way the other parent handled the child turned out to be a better way, would it? Your answer might be "That's not a bad idea. I'll think about it." The question is this: Are you the one who is deciding to change or are you being coerced into change?

Children in Charge

This brings us to another issue that is of great importance. Parents who are going through difficult times, who are struggling with deep emotional conflicts, are sometimes tempted to allow their children to take over, to take care of the parents, to make their own rules. We had an incident in our office a few years ago that made us feel very sad. Mary Ann was a beautiful young woman, bright and articulate, who had recently separated from her husband and was going through a period of self-pity that left her almost dysfunctional. She had come to the office for counseling. Having no one to care for her child, she had asked if she might bring the child along. We were delighted to have little Cara, a charming four-year-old, and the drama that unfolded was very interesting. Mary Ann was relating to us some of the week's events, and at one point she started to cry. Until this point Cara had been sitting on her mother's lap. She gave a long sigh, climbed down, and with a dramatic flourish hurried across the room to get a tissue from the box on the desk. Back she ran and as she wiped her mother's eyes, she turned to us and said, "You know, I have to do this all the time." The incident was not so serious in itself, but it was a clue to what was happening in the relationship. Cara was spending a lot of time comforting her mother, worrying about her mother, even getting up during the night to check on her mother's well-being. Cara was deciding when she would get up, when she would go to bed, and what she would eat. Sometimes she was also making rules for her mother: "Now promise you'll be home by midnight, Mommy." "I don't want you to go out with that Rob any more." This darling little girl was too young to be given this kind of responsibility. She was being robbed of her childhood.

Children get "parentified" in other ways. They may have to do something extraordinary to get parents to stop fighting. For example, they may get in trouble with the police, start drinking, or smoking marijuana. They may do any number of acts that are not usual for them that will somehow change the painful circumstances in which they find themselves. We're not suggesting that all substance abuse can be blamed on warring parents, but it is true that sometimes this is the case. Youth smoke pot or get drunk for many reasons—to be "cool," because it feels good, to be accepted by their peers, among others—but sometimes they become substance users and abusers to escape the pain of their lives.

We see some very sad young people who are frustrated and angry when their parents continue for years with a bitter struggle to get even with each other, to punish each other, and to control each other while their children have to sit by helplessly being more adult than their parents. These children grow up too soon, caught in the middle between two people who profess to love them but whose behavior gives a very different message. Such children learn a lesson in relationship that may be indelible: Don't get married; love turns to hate; children don't matter. Undoubtedly many of the adults who get into this kind of craziness don't intend to hurt their children. They are so involved with their own needs that they fail to see what is happening to their children. They fight for what seem to them to be good reasons: "I'm determined to make him pay for what he has done to me." "I'm fighting for enough money to support these children." "I'm never going to allow someone else to raise my children, and I'll fight with my last breath to get custody," or "I'll kidnap them and she'll never see them again." Some of the reasons for the battle may be valid. The financial burden on a woman who is raising children alone is heavy, and she is entitled to have support, but there are ways to fight that don't have to involve the children. Sometimes the battle may do more harm to the children than being deprived of a high standard of living.

It doesn't hurt children to have to take on extra responsibility after their parents divorce; sometimes it can be beneficial. It may give them a sense of self-worth that they can be helpful at this time. What is harmful is if they become the only responsible members of the family and have to take the major responsibility because their parents have abdicated their role.

Parents who allow their young children to make their own

rules are doing them a disservice. When they are little, children need to be able to trust the people closest to them. One way they learn to trust is by having a parent (at least one) who makes rules and keeps them. Parenting is certainly not just disciplining; it is many other things, too. But discipline is an important part of the parenting task. Parents should take care of children, and only occasionally should young children (in an emergency and for a short period of time) be required to take care of their parents.

Holding On Too Long

Another issue that faces the single parent is how and when to let loose of the children. By being overprotective, by holding on too tightly, the parent may prevent the child from ever being able to make a successful transition out of the family. A parent who is lonely, who has not made a successful adjustment to the single life, and/or who has few friends or other interests may become so dependent on his or her children to supply support and to make the parent feel needed that the parent may hold on to the child by making the child feel guilty about leaving or cause the child to worry about leaving the parent alone. This attachment may be done subtly and even unconsciously, but it does happen. The child may even feel that he or she would be disloyal to leave the family or that the family members, through the trauma of divorce, may have grown so close to one another that it would be difficult for anyone to get out or anyone else to get in.

Parents can help avoid this situation by taking steps to become less dependent on the young people—getting involved with a singles group, making new friends, entertaining more, learning to handle the running of the household alone if necessary (we are not suggesting that family members be allowed to neglect chores regularly). If the parent is able to demonstrate that he or she is perfectly capable of living alone and of enjoying life to the fullest, the children will be freer to live their own lives.

Children can begin when they are very young to make some decisions for themselves. They can decide to wear this pair of jeans or that one; they can decide if they will have toast or an English muffin; they can decide which book they would like to buy. As they get older, they make more decisions that are within their ability to make. Little by little they need to be given an increasing amount of responsibility for their own behavior, always understanding what the limits are. As they prove their ability to be responsible, they earn the right to make more important decisions. If the parent continues to make all decisions for the children as they grow up, they become so dependent that they will never be able to live successfully on their own. A ten-year-old son, for example, can be given the right to decide whether he will do his homework after school or after dinner, but the understanding is that before he goes to bed at the agreed-upon hour, the homework will be done and the parent will check the finished work. After several years of responsible performance, the parent will be able to let this child take full responsibility for getting his work done, with the parent available to help when necessary.

It's interesting how children who grow up in the same home and with the same rules can be so very different. One child might rather die than go to school without the lessons prepared, while another will lay elaborate plans to avoid the homework and fake it through. The responsible one will need much less supervision than the faker, and the faker may be the one who is holding on to the family tenaciously while screaming for freedom!

We sometimes see families where several children have either not married or who have married and divorced within a few years. These may be families in which children have trouble leaving and they are so loyal to the family system that they "never leave home" even if they live hundreds of miles away.

A Reminder

Much of the material in this chapter could be applicable to any family. Just because these kinds of problems arise in a single-parent family doesn't make that family strange or weird. All families have problems, some more severe than others. Even in intact families, children sometimes find themselves in a loyalty bind—where the parents are in a constant tug-of-war for the affection of their children. Many parents exploit their children, and many parents are exploited by their children. Battling married couples hold onto their children as a way of not having to deal with each other. What in the world would they talk about if their children were to leave them? Many children get caught in the middle of this kind of situation, fearing that if they leave, their parents' marriage will fall apart. They are the glue to hold it together.

The point is that although you are having to manage complicated issues, don't get trapped into feeling that everything that happens to your family is because you are a single-parent family. There is no question but that the breakup of a family presents lots of problems. If a child's world falls apart, it would be very strange indeed if he or she didn't show distress. But not all problems are caused by divorce. Many of them are the result of the ordinary struggle that all people have who live in intimate relationship.

EMOTIONS

5

The Pain of It All

"How will the children react?" is a question that arises for almost all parents who are separating. The range of emotions that children experience is not unlike your own, though they have far less experience in handling their feelings than you do. It is helpful to them if you can encourage them to tell you what they are feeling in order that you can be of assistance. Although the list is not exhaustive, these are the common reactions that parents report to us:

Denial—This isn't really happening.
Fear—What's going to happen to me?
Shame—I want to be like other kids who have two parents.
Guilt—I did something to cause my parents' problem.
Confusion—I don't know whom to believe.
Sadness—I can't let myself be happy now.
Depression—It's hopeless.
Hurt—Someone I love has disappointed me.
Blame—One of my parents is responsible for this.
Anger—I'm so frustrated because I can't change anything and it's not fair.

Occasionally parents will report to us that their children have experienced a positive feeling—relief, relief that the hostilities have ceased and that at long last the parents have taken some action to end the tension that has existed in the home.

We believe that you parents have to be the model for helping your children deal with their feelings. If you are a "stiff-upper-lip" kind of person, if you believe that you must model a kind of stoicism for your children and suppress your feelings lest they overwhelm you, then you will not be helping your children to talk about their feelings and find ways to handle them.

There are all kinds of games that parents who separate play with their children. They pretend that everything is okay up until the moment of separation, or they tell the children that Daddy is away on a trip, Mommy is visiting Grandmother, or they make other excuses to delay the moment of truth. You do your children a disservice with these little games. Most of the time they know anyhow or they will hear the truth from someone else, and therefore they come to distrust you. Children are wonderfully resilient. If they are told the truth in an honest, open atmosphere and if they are encouraged to let their feelings be appropriately expressed, they will make it.

You must set the tone for your children. Let them know when you hurt and when you're angry, frustrated, or sad. This openness does not mean that you will drown them in your tears or that you will increase their fears by scaring the daylights out of them every time you hear a noise in the night. A spoonful of courage on your part will help the children to have more courage. If you can assure them that you recognize there are problems to be faced but that together you will find solutions, it will be a great lesson for them in handling other problems in their lives.

Divorce is serious business, not just for the adults involved, but for the children. It would be strange indeed if they did not have some difficult days, if they did not have some strong reactions to having their world torn apart. More than strange, such a situation would be unhealthy. The best you can do is to validate their feelings—"This really hurts you, doesn't it?" "You are feeling very sad today because Daddy isn't here anymore." "I understand that you are angry about what is happening." Reflect to the children what you see in them, rather than asking them always to explain what they are feeling. These are ways of keeping the conversation open, of encouraging them to risk telling you about it without fear that you will put them down.

Tears are a great release for pent-up emotion. Don't tell them to "be brave" when they cry. Obviously there comes a time when the tears need to dry up. If that doesn't happen, then you may be dealing with something more difficult than normal grief, and you will have to seek help from a professional.

If their anger causes children to carry on in ways that are unacceptable and inappropriate, you will have to take measures to help them find other ways to express it. Kicking your sister because you are angry with your father is inappropriate and unacceptable.

There's nothing wrong with letting your children know what you are feeling. There's nothing wrong with letting them know you feel angry with your spouse, sad because he or she left, and frustrated because you can't seem to do anything about it. But there is something very wrong with character assassination of your spouse: "Your father is such a rotten, dirty so and so, and I hate his guts!" is not the way for you to express your anger appropriately. Describe the *feeling* you are having: "I feel so angry when he doesn't send the check on time!" "I am so frustrated by her lack of caring!" And you can encourage the children to express feelings by telling them when you are happy, too: "It's a beautiful day today, and I feel so glad to be alive!" "I feel so grateful to have so many people who love and care about us—Grandma and Grandpa and Charlie and. . . ." The message here is that we are still loved, even if it seems that this important person in our lives has stopped loving us.

Don't expect that your children will be willing to tell you what they are feeling if you are unwilling to tell them what is happening with you. You must trust them if they are to trust you.

Let's talk about some of the specific emotional reactions that we have mentioned and try to describe some of the ways in which they may be manifested by the children.

Denial

We have already mentioned the possibility of parents playing games with children and not letting them know the truth about separation. This kind of activity encourages the children not to believe that their parent has left, and they will foster their own fantasies about it. They will pretend, especially younger children, that Daddy will be home soon. They sometimes even act this out with a doll. They will make up excuses to their friends about why their parent is no longer at home. Older children are more apt to pretend that they don't even notice, or they will take a who-cares? attitude. Your honesty is important in this matter, and you need to help them to accept the truth in any way you can. Emphasize the adjustments you are making and the help the children must give you to cope with the situation. If you can provide them with some action, some participation in coping, they will be more apt to accept the inevitable and to begin to work on adjustment.

Fear

Most children feel more secure with two parents in the house, especially at night. Usually they feel that Daddy will handle any scary situation and if he is not there, they need reassurance that Mom can take care of things. The fears of physical harm are usually minor ones; the real, more serious fears arise from the unknown future. The questions that most commonly arise are: "What will happen to me? Will my remaining parent abandon me, too?" We mentioned in chapter 2 the need to be prepared to answer the question of what will happen to the children when the separation takes place. It helps if the custodial parent will repeat many times over that he or she is dependable, will not leave the child, will return on time or will call, and the like. During the transition period it helps to have the custodial parent be especially aware of these fears and to make life as predictable as possible. For very young children you may want to do some things that will help them to feel more secure—add a night light, let them have a pet in the room at night, or anything within reason that seems to make them feel better. You might show them the locks on windows, the dead-bolt locks on doors (if you don't have such locks, you should under any circumstances). Explain to them the safety rules of the house and what to do in case of fire or other emergency; make sure you have smoke alarms throughout the

house and explain the way they work. You can do a great deal to reduce the fears that children have by calmly and purposely talking about them.

Shame

In spite of the fact that we live in a society where as many as 50 percent of all marriages will end in divorce, there is still a real shame factor involved for many people. Shame is increased for children by having the family whisper about the divorce, by the shame felt by the parents, and by the teasing that other children do. Here again, the children's reaction is often a reflection of the parents' attitude. If the parents can accept the fact that they have thought through all of the alternatives, have tried their best to make the marriage work, and have found that they cannot, then they need to acknowledge divorce as the only acceptable alternative and face it squarely. You can communicate your reasoning to the children and give them the language to use with their friends.

Guilt

Guilt is an emotional reaction that helps persons explain something they don't understand. "I must have caused this to happen." "It must be my fault—there's no other way to explain it." Parents may try to help the child by saying over and over that the child was in no way to blame for what happened. But sometimes the child may know this is not true. They may have heard the parents arguing about the fact that the children come first, that one parent has to spend too much time with the children and the other parent feels neglected. Even when there is no basis for the child's guilt, it may be there anyhow. One of the things that parents can do that may help is to encourage children to understand the difference between things they can change and things they cannot.* Blaming themselves for something over which they have no control will not help to change the situation. You can encourage them to let go of feelings that are not productive and try to concentrate on things they can change.

*For an excellent discussion of the causes of guilt feelings in children of divorce, see *The Parents Book About Divorce*, by Richard A. Gardner, M.D. (New York: Doubleday and Co., Inc., 1977), pp. 138-148.

Confusion

Much of the busyness that is necessary at the beginning of a separation brings a good deal of confusion to all concerned. It comes from trying to work out living arrangements, visitation agreements, new schedules, and all of the many changes that accompany the separation of one parent from the home. Some of this is unavoidable. You yourself are feeling confused much of the time. There is so much to think about that at times you must feel overwhelmed. The best you can do is to keep the children informed of what is happening and what you intend to do about it, so that they begin to feel that things are going to improve.

Sadness

We remember well one eight-year-old whose mother had brought him to see us. He looked so dejected; he refused to smile even when we provided him with some interesting toys. His play with a puppet provided some clues to his mood, for he spoke his feelings through the puppet (a child), explaining to the audience that the child was feeling so sad because his father didn't love him and he had gone away to live with some other children. Mark's (the eight-year-old's) own father had indeed left Mark and was now living with a woman who had children from a former marriage. Through the puppet, Mark explained that he cried sometimes and felt as if he should never laugh anymore because people would not understand how sad he was. He was feeling sorry for himself and probably wanting someone to reassure him that everything was going to be all right. This time of sadness is not usually very serious; it is one way of the child grieving for the past and for the loss of the presence of someone dear to him or her. Quite different is the matter of depression.

Depression

Depression in children is marked by one or several symptoms: loss of appetite, loss of concentration, difficulty in sleeping, rejection of companionship, and signs of withdrawal, listlessness, and irritability. There are many other symptoms which sometimes are indications of depression (such as boredom, excessive sleeping, attitude of hopelessness). If your child's sadness seems to go on for too long a time or if he or she appears to be getting worse with each day, you should not hesitate to call for help. Suicide among children is growing, though rarely among children under twelve. This is not to say that every depressed child is apt to commit suicide, but the possibility is not something that can be ignored or ruled out. Severely depressed children should be referred to psychiatric help. No amount of attention or caring on the part of loving parents is apt to touch this situation.

Hurt

Though we sometimes use the word "hurt" when we mean anger, children do hurt and hurt deeply when someone they love has let them down and has given them reason to feel that they are not loved. The parent who leaves children and then fails to contact them regularly, who disappoints them over and over, and who makes promises that are not kept is a parent who inflicts pain and hurt on those children. They find this kind of treatment very hard to understand. Children give their love freely to their parents when they are little, and they are expected to continue to do so. When that love seems not to be reciprocated, they feel betrayed and that hurts. The parent who thoughtlessly hurts a child is depriving himself or herself of one of life's greatest joys. Children may have to hurt, and you may not be able to spare them from it. Just as you must walk through your own pain, so must they, but it helps a lot to have someone stand beside you, cuddle you when you cry, and tell you that he or she understands.

Blame

Most of us are apt to blame someone when something terrible happens to us. How else can we explain the situation? If one parent wants the divorce and the other does not, it is easy for children to blame the parent who initiates the action. "If you would let Daddy come home, we could all be together," they may say. "It's your fault. You started it," they may angrily accuse. This pattern is more apt to happen as a reflection of what they hear from the parent whom they perceive to be the underdog. Or it may come from hearing both parents blaming each other for the situation, scapegoating each other in order to be the "good guy." Blaming happens in so many cases that one might wish there were some way to bring some sense to the adults who continue to perpetuate it. Blaming is not nearly so apt to happen if both the adults involved will sit down with the children and help them to see that both parents were involved in the decision and that both were part of what happened. The children may still blame both of you for not having the strength to work through your problems (as you tell them to do), but the best you can hope for is that someday when they are involved in intimate relationships they will come to understand the complexity of marriage and will perhaps forgive you.

Anger

Anger has many faces, and some of them are more easily recognizable than others. Religious teachings have convinced some people that to be angry is "sinful" and they must find ways to repress their angry thoughts as well as angry deeds. In fact, anger is a healthy emotion, a very useful one, for it permits one to prepare for defense in case of danger. All of the body's systems rally to prepare for battle. When anger is suppressed because of the conviction that one must not be angry, sometimes anger comes out in other ways. We cry, become anxious, have bad dreams, or develop bodily ailments such as ulcers, headaches, and backaches. Children, like adults, often deny that they are angry. They will scream their denial at the top of their lungs, or they will become sullen or refuse to talk at all.

Children whose parents are divorcing have reason to be angry. They are caught in the middle of something they cannot do anything about, and their parents may be destroying each other with their bitterness. The children may feel abandoned by one of their parents, and the other parent may have become so depressed that the children have in effect lost both of their parents. The children want their lives to be without turmoil, they want their homes to be like the ideal ones they see on TV, or at least they want their family to have two parents like other kids do. When that can't happen, their frustration reaches a high level, and they begin to manifest some of the symptoms described before.

What can you do about their anger? Acknowledge their anger and help the children to find appropriate ways to express it. Help them to identify the real source of their anger and to try to take some kind of action to change what they can. We know many custodial parents who say to us that they feel it is unfair that their children vent their anger on the parent who is taking care of them, who is faithful to them, but never say anything to the noncustodial parent who may be the source of their frustration. The problem is that most of us vent our anger in a safe place. It may be a kind of backhanded compliment to you, but if your children let you have it with both barrels when they are angry with the absent parent, it may be because they trust you and realize that they can tell you how they are feeling and you won't leave them, whereas if they tell the other parent, they may see less of that parent than they now do.

Another way you can help your child who is angry is to think about what you can do to change your own behavior. Are you increasing the problem by being angry yourself a great deal of the time? Are you forever burdening the child with every little detail of the war which you and your spouse are waging? There may be some ways you can think of that will calm the situation somewhat and thereby help your child to feel less frustrated. We remember one father who told his angry son to go in the bathroom, get in the shower, and scream as loud as he wanted to, use whatever language he felt appropriate, but that he would not allow the child to scream at him when his mother was the object of his anger. He also, of course, had encouraged the child to tell his mother how he felt about what was happening and how he felt about some of the things she was doing. But when the child seemed to get more and more agitated, the father had found it helped his son to do something concrete. Hence, he suggested the shower to provide enough noise so that no one else in the house had to listen.

Summary

Your child may exhibit none of the feelings that we have talked about in this chapter. He or she may have some other ways of expressing the pain of separation. But even when children deny pain, even if they seem to be perfectly well adjusted, the pain is there, and sooner or later they will have to deal with it. We see many adults who for a long time have anticipated being free of a painful marriage, and they think that they will rejoice and celebrate when the day finally comes. Almost all of the people we have known in this situation have found to their surprise that they still had some powerful emotions to overcome. If nothing else, we all sorrow for what might have been when life brings us the pain of separation.

6

The Creative Power
of Rootedness

When Alex Haley's *Roots* was published in 1976, it became an
overnight bestseller, and its popularity has continued to this
day. The television version of the book drew one of the largest
audiences in the history of that medium. Not only was Haley's
story well told, it reminded all who saw it of their own family
history, and the interest that the book aroused in genealogy
created a whole new industry. Hundreds of books on family
research have flooded the market.

Most of us grew up in families not knowing or caring anything about all of those people who preceded us. We heard
family stories from our parents and grandparents. They were
amusing, sometimes boring, but for the most part we didn't
think much about our family history. We fought with our parents about rules—family laws—but in truth the rules were in
themselves a kind of security. We could depend on our parents
to follow those rules which formed the structure for our lives.
We felt, rather than thought about, the family as a place of
security, a refuge, a place where, as Robert Frost described it,
"they have to take you in." Others have described the family
as a "living laboratory of human relationships," where we try

out all of our emotions and learn to trust in order to be prepared to trust the world.

When one of the parents leaves the home, that security is apt to be severely shaken. "Who am I?" This usual cry for personal identification may be the question raised by the children of divorce when they feel there is no longer a family where they belong.

All of us seek community; we want to belong. Even the youth who ran from their families in the sixties sought to belong. They formed communities or small groups which very much resembled families. Some of them entered such groups immediately upon leaving their families of origin. An important task of the custodial parent in a divorce situation is to help the children feel that they are still in a family, that there is a stream of history of which they are an important part. This connectedness is not easy in a society that insists on calling yours a "broken" or "split" family. The emphasis should not be on the brokenness but on the family, for in many cases there is less brokenness after divorce than before, particularly in those families where there has been a great deal of conflict. You are still a family, even if one member is no longer living in the home. Helping your children to feel that they belong to something, that they are a vital part of the family, and that they can trust you, will give them the kind of foundation for life that you want them to have.

Discipline as Security

We often ask ourselves when we are seeing a family, "Who is in charge of this family?" Sadly, we must sometimes conclude that the smallest member of the family is in control. The parents seem unable or unwilling to set any limits for the children. They will often claim that they don't know how to control, but in most cases they mean they are afraid to control. Such parents are sometimes afraid that their children will not love them if they set down rules of conduct; they need the children so much that they can't risk losing them by any act that seems unfriendly. The single parent is most often worried about rules for the children. He or she may have self-doubts about the fairness of the rules, recognize that help is not available to implement the rules, and fear the ability of the children to threaten the parent ("I'll go live with my dad. He wouldn't do that to me")—all of these become hazards to the single parent.

The authors don't believe that "children want discipline" necessarily, at least not consciously. Most children we know would fight like tigers to avoid rules, but rules are a very important part of children's development. It is a way they learn trust: "My parents will not allow me to . . . "; this is trust that the parents will stand firm on what they have promised. For this reason, it is very important that parents set down only those rules that they are prepared to carry through. Threats mean nothing. Children learn at a very early age how to make the parents bend. We can remember a five-year-old who didn't want to wear boots to school. His mother told him he either had to wear them or stay out of puddles. He wasn't out of sight of the house when he encountered a most inviting puddle left by a recent shower. He stood there looking at it for a minute, gave a quick glance over his shoulder, and then went through it, stomping hard enough to wet his trousers to the knees. You could almost hear the wheels turning as he thought, "She doesn't mean it."

One of the most effective teachers in our area had a wonderful system of discipline. She taught first grade. Within minutes, it seemed, on the very first day of class she had established the rules for that classroom. She never yelled, she was very soft-spoken, and every child who attended her classes thought she was wonderful. Her classroom was bright and cheery; there were soft animals and fluffy pillows; the chairs were painted happy colors by the teacher herself; hers was the happiest classroom in the school. But she was tough. Her students knew that when she stood in "her" circle, she wanted their attention, and she got it. When it was time to clean up, they cleaned up because she played a musical clue on the piano; she didn't have to tell them. The extra bonus at the end of every day and many times throughout the day was a kiss or a hug and a word of encouragement.

Be tough, but be fair in disciplining your children. Be consistent as everyone says, but don't knock yourself over the head if you are inconsistent sometimes. No one achieves it completely, but consistency is what we all need to strive for.

The Family Legacy

In order to help your children understand their family legacy, you may have to do some hard work to understand it yourself. How much do you know about your parents' childhood? How much do you know about your grandparents' childhood? How much do you understand of the dynamics of your relationship with your siblings and your parents? This historical understanding may take some doing, but the place to begin is with your parents. To do this kind of work will bring you several benefits. You will feel more connected to your parents as you understand how they got to be who they are. You will understand why they did some of the things that you experienced in growing up. They will feel flattered that you are interested in their lives, their families, and your asking to hear more will be a gift of love to them. Reconnecting with your family will provide you with a resource for your own adjustment period, and it will prepare you to talk with your children about their heritage. At the end of this chapter is a list of questions you may want to use in your discussions with your parents. They are questions that will help them to tell you more of the feelings they had in growing up. What you want to know is not merely a description of what the world was like when they were growing up, but rather how it felt to them as a boy or girl growing up in that family. The question we often use is, "How was it for you when you were growing up?" Answers to this kind of question are much more apt to help you understand your parents and even to allow you to forgive them for some of the things that they did. If they are willing, it would be fun to put your interview on tape. Wouldn't you like to have that kind of record of your own grandparents and great grandparents?

An important thing to remember as you think about giving your children a feeling of rootedness is that they have two sides to their family legacy. They need to know more about the other side also. This two-sided history may be difficult for you to obtain if you and your former spouse are not on good terms. You may even feel that you would just as soon the children forgot all about the other side. If the children see their other parent regularly, it may be possible that you could encourage them to ask the parent to help them to research that side of their family. No matter how much you dislike your former spouse's family, it is part of your children's heritage and they are entitled to know about it. Listen to a man in his fifties:

All my life I had connected with my father's side of the family. When my mother died, I was only two and I never heard my father speak of my mother or her family in my life. I was raised by my father's mother and knew that side very well. There were many things about my father that I found hard to accept, and yet I feared that I would be just like him. Somewhere along the way, not many years ago, it finally occurred to me that I was my mother's son also, and I began a desperate search for some way to get to know who she was. This was a great revelation to me and a very important one.

Turning to face one's parents and hearing their side may help you to understand yourself better. And this insight could be an important factor in your adjustment. One woman told us:

My father was an alcoholic, and I grew up resenting him for his behavior. He was not available to me at a very important time in my life and it made me very distrustful of men. When I finally heard his side and learned of the terribly deprived life he had had, I was able to understand why he found solace in a bottle. It had been his way of avoiding pain. How glad I am that I was able to do this before he died because we are now good friends and he has added a great deal to my life.

Looking more closely at who that other parent is may provide some important healing for your children. They don't have to excuse irresponsible behavior, but they may better understand why the other parent has acted as he or she did. That understanding may help to relieve them of the feeling that the separation of their family is somehow the fault of the children.

One's relational legacy may not be very pleasant to ponder. It may be very painful to face the relationships that have shaped the course of your life, but looking at them is the first step to making a decision to upgrade the legacy. If you can see a negative pattern through several generations, you may decide that this is one place where you can work hard to change it. Suppose, for example, you see evidence that the family has been so tightly bound that people have trouble becoming adults, in separating from the family. You will be alerted to the need to help your children to become more independent and for you to become less dependent. Such dependence on a spouse can be suffocating and may have a negative factor in your marriage. Everyone has some negative patterns in his or her family and the way to change them to more positive patterns is to recognize that they are there.

Every family also has many positive patterns of relationship. A woman we know asked her mother to tell her shortly before she died, what her family was like. She thought a few minutes and said, "They were honest, God-fearing rebels, and Democrats!" And she said it with pride. There was no question in her mind about what her family stood for. Jewish families have for generations had a tradition of writing an ethical will. These wills accompanied the legal documents which distributed the family's assets and properties. They were probably the antecedents of our "Last Will and Testament." We still write our wills, but few of us include the "testament" anymore. Ethical wills exhorted the children to carry on the family traditions both in religious practice and in everyday life. They laid a heavy responsibility on parents to take care of their children, to see to their education and their behavior; they addressed the matter of husband-wife relationships; they held up the value of honesty, truthfulness, fairness, and justice. These wills included instructions for conducting oneself in business and in one's personal life. In reading one of these ethical wills, it is clear that the writer feels very strongly the burden of passing on to his children the description of what the family believes in, what its members stand for. You can feel the power of that kind of family structure; the children would have no doubt about their belonging.

You may want to think about these issues. What do you believe in? What are you willing to stand for? What are the values that you want to pass on to your children?

Traditions as Roots

One of the hardest things for families to handle after a divorce is what to do about the established traditions, especially around holidays. "We always . . . ," "Remember the time. . . ." These phrases bring painful memories, painful because the occasion will never be quite the same, and every time a holiday comes around, the memories have to be faced again.

Some families have found a way to deal with this by deciding to establish new traditions. Look into the ethnic or national background of your family and try to find out what some of the more ancient traditions were. What did they do on holidays? Were there special foods that were cooked? What was the Christmas holiday like? or the Hannukkah celebration? Was it different in years past? What kinds of games did they play? Katherine, reflecting on her family, said:

Our children have always been so disappointed that we have so little variety in our national background—other kids are Irish or German or something much more interesting than simply English. We did a little digging and found that there might be some American Indian blood in the family, and that expanded the possibility for more interesting traditions. Then we simply decided that we would borrow a few from our friends. Some Italian friends had a lovely tradition for Easter. On Easter morning each child had a home-baked circle of bread on his plate; in the center was a colored egg still in the shell, and pieces of dough had been laid over the egg in the form of a cross. The egg was colored before baking and when it was baked with the bread, it was hard-cooked. Our children loved these little breads, and now we look forward to having them every year.

On the other hand, because so many of our ancestors were English, we decided that we would learn more about traditional English dishes and customs and would try to incorporate them into our holiday festivities. We learned to enjoy Yorkshire pudding, and from Grandma's cookbook we made plum pudding, raisin pie, and English trifle.

A very creative friend told us about some of the things her family does every year. For example, at Halloween they spread a tablecloth over the table (a big cloth that hangs down to the floor), and they all get underneath and have a "spooky" supper together, using only an electric candle for light. There are all kinds of possibilities for the kinds of food you might serve— witchburgers, goblin pudding made with corn, or black cat shapes for chocolate ice cream. The children would love to help you think of creative ways to plan a menu to celebrate the occasion.

Another idea of the same friend is appealing. She takes the family to a nearby state park for a winter picnic. They build a fire and have hot dogs, and every year they talk about whether it's colder this year than last. "Remember the time it snowed, and we nearly froze?"

The important thing is that you let your mind soar; think about ways to create some new traditions, things that other people don't do that can have your own distinctive stamp on them. Maybe you'll decide one snowy day that the family will take advantage of the weather and maybe play Monopoly all day on the living room floor and not even get out of your bathrobes all day long. Ask yourself what you remember most fondly about your childhood. You will undoubtedly think about the fun times, the crazy times you had together. There's no reason why that has to stop now, just because one member of the family is no longer with you.

An older mother, reflecting on her children's teenage years, says:

Our kids can't look at a spray can of whipped topping without instantly recalling the battle two of them had. It started slowly, with the eldest deciding to shoot a little squirt of cream down his sister's back. She remembered that there was another can in the refrigerator, and in a minute the battle was on. The kitchen was a mess, and before it was over we all had to take a shower, but what fun we had!

Another time we read somewhere that it was possible to hang a spoon on your nose, and we decided to try it. (It's easy. Simply breathe on the inner bowl of the spoon, rub it gently on your nose, and pretty soon it will hang there for several minutes.) This became such a tradition in our family that even with the most inhibited of our guests, we were teaching them the skill.

Documenting the Happy Times

Here is a report of what one person has done for her daughter:

When our oldest daughter was married, I wanted to give her something very special as a wedding present, but we hadn't much money at the time. I couldn't think about some elaborate gift that would cost a lot. I have always thought that my most creative periods came during those times in my life when I was the poorest. It is so much easier to purchase something than to take the time and effort to create it. Molly had been a very special girl, always so very thoughtful of others, and I fretted for a long time in trying to think of what her special gift would be.

Finally, I decided to write a book for her. It was a lot of fun, and it was good therapy for me in letting go of her. I included a lot of pictures, and the pictures helped me to remember things I had forgotten. The book begins with the feelings I experienced when I first knew I was pregnant. It includes stories about family friends and how her grandparents and her father and brother welcomed her into the family. It relates her physical characteristics to those of her relatives on both sides of the family. It reminds her of places we lived, of vacation experiences, of silly as well as serious incidents. It includes the names of doctors, of ministers, of teachers, and others who had a part in her life. It recalls family pets and their fate; it includes the joys that she brought to us along the way, as well as some of the messes that she got into. The book ends with her sixteenth birthday party, to which she was allowed to invite as many as she wished.

After that year it seemed to me that she knew more about her life than I did, and so I urged her to continue her life story as she began her own family. Thus she could provide a history which could be handed down through the years, generation to generation. With the birth of her first child she had done just that, and she has told me over and over how important "her book" has been to her.

You don't need to be especially skilled at writing to do this kind of thing. The book is for no one but your children, and they don't care that you're not a great writer. Many of your own local expressions (from West Virginia, Brooklyn, Maine, and so forth) may be used in the book and, your children will enjoy them even if they tease you about them. That's who you are and that's a part of your children's legacy. Your only regret will be that you didn't start sooner, because of the many things you may leave out.

Writing this kind of record of your children's life can be an interesting thing to do. The earlier you start on such a project the more material you will be able to collect. The book will help the children to remember what life was like before their mother or father left, and it can be a great booster of self-esteem. Imagine how you would feel if your parent had written a whole book just about you. Many single parents tell us that the hardest thing they have to face after a separation is the long hours of loneliness. They are accustomed to having someone with whom they share their free time, and now the weekends stretch before them like a wasteland. We would urge you to decide that you will use your time creatively in a creative solitude which can be very beneficial. Instead of focusing so much on your self and your own needs and instead of slipping into a pattern of self-pity, decide that you will be concerned about the needs of your children. Spend as much time as you can creating an atmosphere of security and joy for them. Actually this creative parenting can be of great value to you in your own adjustment. There is an important side effect that comes in doing good things for someone you love. You usually get back more than you give.

We're not suggesting that you think only of the children. Of course you have to think about yourself. Certainly you need time to heal, and that may require some outside help to provide you with the perspective and objectivity that is very difficult to attain at this time. It may be that the best kind of professional help will be addressed to the whole family, not just one member. All of you are adjusting, and how you relate to each other, how you help each other, is important.

Extended Family

Members of your extended family can be very helpful in giving the children a sense of their belonging. Grandparents can make a real contribution, in more ways than providing financial help or simply baby-sitting. Most parents want to support their children through times of difficulty, but often they don't know how, especially if they don't live close to you. They might, for example, purchase a book for a child, read the book into a tape recorder, and then give the child the book and the tape. Even young children can learn how to operate a tape recorder, and it need not be an expensive one. Then the child can turn the pages of the book while he or she listens to the grandparent read. Think what a relief it would be to have some of these tapes and books on hand for the child to use while you are cooking dinner!

We recognize, too, that there are times when grandparents can do great harm to the children they love. They can, for instance, get in the way of children seeing their other grandparents by making negative remarks about "your father's parents." The two sets of grandparents can get into a tug-of-war in an effort to prove who is the better grandparent. This kind of craziness can be cut short by a parent who will stand firm with both sides of the family to let them know that you do not approve of what they are doing and to insist that if the children are to see them, they must stop exploiting the children in this way. Children, even grown-up children, should not have to chose between their grandparents, any more than they should have to choose one parent over the other.

Grandparents are an important part of the child's life; they add a dimension that is not available anywhere else. We would urge strongly that you find ways for the children to be able to enjoy both of their parents' families. Perhaps you will have to take the initiative to let the grandparents know what is appropriate and what is not. It is not appropriate for either side to make derogatory remarks about the other, or to try to prevent the children from seeing both parents' relatives. From our point of view, the parent most preferred to have custody of children is that parent who is most willing to see to it that the children have access to both parents. If grandparents continue to do and say things which make life difficult for the children, then it may be that you will have to decide to limit their access. If one of the parents engages in this kind of destructive behavior, then you may have to appeal to the courts.

It is so important for the children to feel connected with all of their family that we would urge you to include the grandparents in some family counseling sessions in order to help them to understand how they can continue to have good relationships with their grandchildren in ways that will be positive for all concerned. Most grandparents really want to do what is best for the children, but sometimes they have trouble understanding what that is.

Changing Names

Once in a while we encounter a female client who, though she is not remarrying, decides to change her name back to her maiden surname. This change can be difficult for her children:

> I was so fed up with my former husband that I wanted to wipe out all connection with him. My parents were delighted when I told them I was going to resume my maiden name. I was astonished to learn the reaction of my children. They are all in their teens, and it had not occurred to me that they would care at all. They acted as if I were abandoning them. "We're the Arnolds," they said, "and you're acting like you don't want to be one of us."

She finally decided not to change her name, realizing how important it was to the children. The name problem sometimes arises with a second marriage, but usually the children can come to accept this change as a legal necessity rather than simply a psychological symbol for their mother. You may want to think about the significance of returning to your maiden name as an act of loyalty to your family of origin, and whether or not it may indicate your difficulty in separating from that family, which could have been a factor in the failure of the marriage.

Changing Residence

Some judges are very sensitive to the needs of children, and they make every effort to allow the children to continue their lives with as little change as possible following the separation of their parents. Most judges recognize that the separation itself may be traumatic enough, especially to very young children, and they will, when possible, insist that the custodial parent with the children be allowed to remain in the house and thus provide some measure of stability for the children. When this is not possible, both parents should be sensitive to providing some measure of rootedness as symbolized by the surroundings. Rene Dubos, in his wonderful book *A God Within,** refers to the "spirit of place." The parent who attempts to continue the spirit of the home in which the child feels secure will be making a real contribution to the child's successful transition. This continuing spirit requires some effort, but the rewards are worth that effort. Maintaining the familiar patterns of mealtime, of bedtime routine, of church attendance, of play together—all help the children to feel that they are loved and that life can go forward happily.

Suggested Questions for Family Investigation

These are the kinds of questions you will want to ask your parents, grandparents, or other relatives in order to get a fuller picture of your family and the way they related to one another.

1. Obtain specific information about the way the family was structured and the atmosphere prevailing when they were growing up.
   What were your parents like?
   What did they do for you?
   Were they able to provide security and safety as you grew up?

2. Obtain information from each parent, one at a time. For example, ask your mother:
   What was your mother like? What was her personality like? What did she look like?
   What did she expect of you? What did you get from her? What things did you do together?
   Were you closer to your mother or your father?
   Was your relationship always the same with your mother? Did it change as you grew up? How is it now?
   (Ask similar questions about your mother's father. Then get information from your father about his parents.)

*Rene Dubos, *A God Within* (New York: Charles Scribner's Sons, 1972), p.22.

3. Get detailed information about the brothers and sisters, relationships to one another and to your parent or the other person whom you are interviewing. Be sure to ask about feelings—for example:
   Did you think you were treated fairly in the family?
   Was someone else the favorite?
   How did you feel about yourself when you were little?

4. Ask the person to tell you how he or she feels about his or her marriage (divorce, separation, number of children, abortions, miscarriages, and so forth). Pay attention to how the person reacts to your questions and then make note of these reactions.

5. Ask the person: How did your parents feel about your marriage?

6. How did you separate from your parents?

7. Ask about any deaths in the family and how the family handled death. This will help you to get some clues as to how the family handles loss of any kind—money, possessions, divorces.

8. What family laws or slogans do you remember?

9. What values did the family hold?

10. What family stories do you remember that your parents told you?

11. Did your family talk about feelings? Did you know when your parents were hurting, worried, or sad? Was it all right to express anger?

12. How did the family handle conflict?

13. Did you touch each other? Was there much kissing and hugging? What made you feel loved or unloved?

14. Who did the disciplining? Who handled the money?

7

Noncustodial Parenting

We are constantly amazed by the fact that we meet so many people, chiefly males, who feel that because they don't have custody of their children, they are no longer parents. Very few males who are single parents enroll in our parenting classes. They somehow get the idea that because their spouse has the major role in parenting, they have little or no significance in their children's lives. This is simply not so.

Weekend parenting is difficult at best, but children need to feel that both their parents care about them, and they surely can benefit from a continuing relationship with both male and female parents. This relationship is just as true for girls with their fathers and boys with their mothers as it is for parents and children of the same sex.

For this relationship to have the highest value, it is important that both parents work at making the visitation a good experience. The custodial parent can help the noncustodial parent to do a better job by keeping him or her informed about the children's progress in school, about any fears they are experiencing, about special health needs, household chores, rules for behavior, and so on. Again, communication and cooperation are required between the parents, and a willingness on the part of both is necessary to be sure that they put aside their own anger with each other when dealing with the children. The very fact that you are reading this book would indicate that you are concerned about your children's welfare, and so we are going to assume goodwill on your part. If what you find here seems to make sense to you, invite your former spouse to read the book. Then perhaps you can work together at least in this one area.

Keeping in Contact

The noncustodial parent should provide the children with all the information they need to be able to reach the parent— telephone numbers at work and at home, hours when it would be most convenient for the child to call, schedules of trips or vacations, any pertinent information that will help the children to feel the parent is available. If you have to be away for any length of time, plan to telephone your children or send them a card, a note, or a letter. Getting mail is a thrill to any child, and it takes very little time to write a note. It is also a very inexpensive way of keeping in touch. Buy a supply of cards so that you don't have to go to the store so often. Make a note of interesting things that you encounter in your daily routine; then when the time comes to write, you will be able to say something of interest. "I saw something today that reminded me of you," or "Something happened today that I thought you would enjoy"—these are the kinds of things that make your children believe that you think about them when you are not with them.

Birthdays Are Important! Some people grew up in families where there was little attention given to birthdays, but there are few people who don't remember their own birthdays. Children are accustomed to going to birthday parties for their friends, and they look forward to their own with great anticipation. Find some way to remind yourself of your children's birthdays far enough in advance that you can make arrangements to be there and to provide a gift. It need not be the most expensive gift in the world; it is much more important that it be something into which you put some thought. You remembered that your son loves bright colors ... you know of his interest in model airplanes . . . you notice that he loves to have things with his name on them. Perhaps you plan a special outing that pleases the child—you may arrange to take the child camping in suitable weather. This unusual activity may take some doing, and it will require that you check it out with the custodial parent, but whatever you plan, the child will be pleased because you took the trouble to think about it and make the arrangements. The most successful weekend parents we know are those who take the job seriously enough that it is a number one priority with them, and they allow themselves to enjoy their children rather than regard the whole occasion as a chore to be done.

What Do We Do When It Rains?

What to do on those weekend visits is a recurring problem for all noncustodial parents. We hear stories about the "Santa-Claus syndrome" in which the parent does nothing but shower gifts on the children every time they visit. Fortunately, these parents are in the minority. We believe that most weekend parents want to do a good job, but they find it very difficult when they are living in an apartment with little space for having more than a minimum of activity. They try to get outside as much as possible for activities, but if it rains, then what? After a few weeks of visitation, the local museums and other places to visit have become old hat. Now what?

The most important thing for you to remember is that the children need to feel that you are sharing yourself with them, not simply entertaining them. They want you to be genuinely interested in what is going on with them, not just going through the motions.

Suppose you let them help you plan a meal that they like, and then you go out together to buy the food, bring it home, and prepare it together. Even small children can participate in this. Although they will probably tell you they'd rather go to a fast-food restaurant, going out to eat is not going to provide much interaction between you. The same is true of going to the movies. You don't talk to each other at the movies or when you are watching television. Most children will sit in front of the tube like zombies if they are bored, but they will leave it gladly if you have something more interesting for them to do.

You have to learn to be creative. It's easy to say, "I don't know what to do. How do I know what the kids want?" Check out books for parents in the local library and see what they suggest. Talk with other parents and find out what they do with their children. Make up something—if the weather is nice, go out for a roll down the hill. There's nothing wrong with a soggy picnic provided you are dressed suitably and the food is easy to eat.

One of the best picnics I can remember as a child was when we had to crawl back under an overhanging boulder to get out of the rain. We decided to eat there, and it was loads of fun. We made up stories about being Indians and thought about how they lived in the-out-of-doors most of the time.

Other Ideas for Activities

- Ask your child's teacher about the kinds of books that would be good for your child at his or her particular age and developmental level.
- Take the child to the library. Custodial parents seldom have time to do this. The library is a storehouse of information and activities. You can borrow records from most libraries, and if you ask, they will help you locate many different things of interest for children to see and do.
- Take the child to the store with you. He or she can make up a list of needed items, help plan nutritious meals, and at the same time learn something about costs. Let the child count the money needed at the check-out counter. Most stores will tolerate the few minutes it takes, and this helps young children learn to handle money.
- Take workshops and seminars on parenting, and read all you can about how to handle children the ages of yours.
- Make something together for the child to take home. It can be something to eat or something to play with. The fact that you worked together on something makes it special.

There is an endless variety of things you might decide to do with older children. Let them know what your limits are so far as cost is concerned, and then insist that they help you decide how you can best spend your time together. Maybe your son or daughter would appreciate learning what you know about repairing a car or baking something like bread. Maybe you want to work on your family history together and learn all you can about how to do this and then continue the process with each visit.

If They Are Reluctant to Visit

The children need to know that their visits are important to you. The reason for a visit is not just that they need you, but you need them also, and they should have this clearly in mind. If they act as if they don't want to come (and this can happen as they grow older and have a lot of their own activities to take up their time), you can empathize with their needs, but let them know that you will work out a plan that will allow them to continue their activities and still allow for your own important visits with them.

One reason why children balk at visitation is that they are feeling strain due to the stress between their parents. Read the chapter on "Children in the Middle" to understand this better. Perhaps you can find a way to relieve the strain.

Be willing to negotiate a schedule of visitation that is workable for all concerned but hold fast to your need to see the children. You are entitled to their relationship and should not relinquish it too easily.

Visiting with Grandparents

It is a good thing for children to continue to see all of their relatives after a divorce, but the visits with the extended family should not be a substitute for spending time with the parent. Too many parents who are uncomfortable with visitation head for their parents' home and plunk the kids there for the entire visiting time. This situation is not fair to the children, for they want to spend time with the parent. Of course, they want to see their grandparents, aunts, uncles, and cousins, but the parent should make sure that these visits are not simply an easy way out of his or her own responsibility.

Other Adult Companions

Particularly in the beginning, it is very difficult for children to accept the presence of other adults (especially adults of the opposite sex) during their time to visit. They feel resentful that the other persons are present, and they will find some way to act out their anger even though they can't find the courage to tell you. Try to be sensitive to their feelings—introduce others to them for a short time and then spend time alone with them. There will be time enough later for you to have others along. Let the children have time to come to terms with the divorce and to give up their hopes that you and your spouse will be reconciled. When you have reestablished a good, trusting relationship with your children, they will be much more receptive to your new companion.

We recognize that most of you will marry again. Children can accept remarriage in time, but it is hard for them if a parent is rushing to the altar within a short time of the divorce. If it is at all possible, give them time to heal before taking the step of remarriage.

Relationship with the School

What is happening with your child at school can be very important to you. There are several things you can do. First of all, it is necessary that you clear your right to contact the school with the custodial parent. Some custody agreements are silent on this matter, but the assumption is that the custodial parent has sole authority over the child's school records. If you and your ex-spouse are working together for the good of the child and if your communication is good, you probably can get permission to contact the school for information that will help you in supporting your child's progress. Make sure that your motives are the right ones. Too many noncustodial parents try to use this as a way to harrass the custodial parent, and it is a despicable thing to do. If your ex-spouse agrees, there are several things that can be arranged:

- Teachers usually are willing to hold separate conferences with noncustodial parents (and even with stepparents).
- Teachers are willing to mail notices about school events to noncustodial parents (it is thoughtful to supply stamped envelopes).
- You can offer volunteer services to the school, which will allow you to see what other children the age of your child are doing—either in her or his class or in a class of the same level.

- You can be a guest speaker at your child's school if you have expertise in an area that fits the school program.

Let the teachers know if there is a lot of bitterness between you and your ex-spouse so that they can be aware of it and not do anything to increase the tension.

Other Dos and Dont's

Do be on time, or else telephone to report that you will be late. Children feel such deep disappointment when they get ready to go out with their parent and the parent is consistently late. They will come to believe that they can't trust you. That is a great loss.

Don't get the children so overtired and excited that they will have difficulty in settling down when they get home. We have teachers who report to us that they can always tell when the child has been to visit the noncustodial parent. It takes the children several days to settle down at school. Take it easy. If you do something especially stimulating, make sure that the child has time to calm down before it is time to return home.

Do check schedules with the custodial parent so that you can coordinate your efforts and make the best·use of your time with the children.

Don't try to be in competition with your former spouse to see who can be the better parent. Consistency in carrying out rules that are made for the children at home is for their benefit. Agreeing to buy things that they don't need, just to buy their affection, is very destructive.

Don't try to play on the children's sympathy because you are having to make sacrifices. It may be very difficult for you at this time—you may be living in a small apartment while the rest of the family continues to live in the nice home. You may have had to give up a lot of the pleasures that you enjoyed before. Your lifestyle may have changed dramatically from that of your spouse and children, but that's not their fault. Children worry about their parents, even when nothing is wrong. If you burden them with your problems, it can make them feel guilty, and that's not fair.

Do understand that the child may need to telephone home. We see a lot of children who are so concerned about what is happening to the custodial parent while they are away that they can't make it through the whole weekend without some contact. Don't be put off by this need. Accept it as normal and your attitude will help to relieve some of the child's anxiety.

Don't worry about everything being perfect for the whole time you are together. Children need to learn that they have to deal with frustrations. That's the real world. So solve problems together; don't try to protect the children from them.

Do try to be flexible in arranging for visitation. Don't insist that the children visit with you simply because it is "your day" when there is something else important that the child wants to do. Of course you have to weigh the importance but try to see the child's view as well as your own.

Don't think you have to see all of the children at the same time. It may work to the whole family's advantage for you to see children separately, particularly when there is a wide age range. You might be able to do some things with older children that would not be possible if a very young child were with you. In addition, it is easier to establish close relationship on a one-to-one basis, and all children enjoy having an exclusive time with a parent.

Do remember that you can help your children build self-esteem. Children of divorce very often feel that they have been divorced as well as their parents. Since they may feel that you have rejected them, it becomes very important for you to let the children know how much you love them. Remember to compliment them for good performance and for achievements, no matter how small. This affirmation should be done genuinely or it will backfire; compliments should fit the accomplishment and should not be given unless earned. Children know when adults are putting them on, and they feel even less self-esteem when this happens.

8

Standing Room

Emergencies tend to bring out our survival powers, even while the mind is saying, "This can't be happening to me!" And so through the most difficult of circumstances, we find a way to make it. Then, when the emergency is over and the reality of the changed circumstances becomes apparent, we realize that we are going to have to find something more permanent and that we need to establish a firm footing under ourselves and for others who depend on us. Gradually we accept the implicit truth that if we are to cope, we are the ones who have to do the coping. In that sobriety, we know within ourselves that a new set of goals will have to come into focus if life is to move on:

I always thought that I did all of the parenting and that he [husband] was so preoccupied with his own things that I could expect nothing from him. But after the first panic that brought me near hysteria, it came to me so clearly—I really was depending on him—even if it was in a negative way, if you know what I mean. He gave me clues, even when he seemed to be withdrawn and hostile, as to what to do and how to do it. I hated to admit it, but I really was dependent on him. Now I see that really facing this by myself is a new experience for me.

Already this young woman is learning that she has to depend on herself. Instead of finding someone else to depend on, she must find some personal "standing room."

By "standing room" we mean a place to strengthen self-confidence, to experience self-fulfillment, to gain a feeling of personal value and a sense that what is started can be finished. The support structures of the past simply aren't enough to supply sufficient undergirding when you are tackling the job of parenting alone.

The ground for personal meaning and competence, the standing room, suggests a basis for life that appears to be religious, but it is a kind of applied religious experience that has not been felt to any great extent so long as everything around has been going well.

In thinking about the thousands of families we have counseled, we could estimate that three-quarters of them have been reasonably active in some religious community prior to the separation or divorce, but of that number, few of them appear to have experience in relating the articles of their faith to the major decisions and shaping experiences of their lives in any conscious way. To affirm that God sustains life, that God's love is a paradigm for love may be affirmed in creedal statements in religious settings without those insights becoming significant factors in the flow of life itself. It is when the press of negative circumstances is upon us and we have to take the religious dynamics into the marketplace of human experience that we realize how "academic" or how "ecclesiastical" our religious faith has been in the past.

Sure, I believed all those things, but I was strong, and I was careful. When I made decisions, I felt that I was making the right decisions; and when I couldn't decide something, all I had to do was wait it out, and things would turn out all right. I never really thought that my religious beliefs literally shaped how I acted.

From the beginning of time, catastrophies and emergencies have threatened dissolution of all that has made sense to a people. Such circumstances have been the occasions for human beings to find new ground for their existence. Thus the eighth-century prophets (Amos, Hosea, and Isaiah of Jerusalem) and the sixth-century prophets (Isaiah, Jeremiah, Ezekiel) faced the destruction of their known worlds, the erosion of meaning, and the dissolution of hope. They searched the depths of their religious faith for a place to stand. Not finding that standing room in the traditional religious responses of their people, they worked it through before God to find meaning, vision, strength, and motivation to discharge their responsibilities to the people. Thus the historic faith of the people grew up out of the destruction of the times. The dynamics are similar for the family and for the individual.

I stopped my self-pity and my tired moanings. I said, "Look at those kids—God has entrusted their right to the fullness of life to you. Shape up! You've got an assignment." And I began to see them and to see myself as never before. I understood in a fresh way what it means that God creates human beings and places them in the hands of those God knows are equal to the task.

In the personal discovery of basic religious faith, the beleaguered parent finds the foundation for building hope and love, and in the process he or she develops a framework for coping. This discovery, as seen in retrospect, is often viewed as the beginning point of vital religious faith.

The religious rituals, the homilies, the Bible stories, the hymns, and even the religious friendships, all took on new meanings for me.

We are not dealing here with religion either as a panacea or as a substitute for the hard work of parenting alone. The discovery of the personal power and perspective through religious faith is seen here as the foundation for the hard work of being a single parent.

The concept of a "standing place" suggests such personal factors as self-composure, self-assurance, the ability to plan ahead, and the willingness to accept and complete heavy responsibilities. But beyond that, the religious ground often becomes the true basis for personal freedom. The imprisonment by the daily agenda has to be broken open. One has to find a new direction when the demands on the present life appear fixed from the outside and the human spirit is tempted to accept entrapment.

The simple understanding of the self from the religious perspective focuses on the self as created in the image of God—free, creative, responsible. A woman, after one of our mountain retreats, exclaimed:

> I remember that day out there on the riverbank when we discovered Psalm 139. It really registered with me that God not only knows everything about me—even before I was born—but also everything about my children before they were born. I felt the strongest sense of relief when that meaning came to me. I don't have to go on hiding, nor cringing, nor pretending. I can be myself; God knows me and is with me. The load simply slipped off my shoulders.

Making a Claim for Oneself

Finding standing room also means being willing to make a claim for oneself, because the nurtured parent is more able to nurture children. This self claim is not a matter determined by clocks and calendars. A man who has parented three children alone for the past four years (ages now thirteen, eleven, and eight), said that he had gained understanding all right, but it didn't take away what he has to face when he comes home from work. Five days a week he comes home with his head filled with dinner plans, getting ready to listen to what happened at school, settling arguments, doing chores, helping with homework, playing some games, not to mention getting set to cope with unexpected needs, emergencies, group meetings, and illness. But he says:

> Before I understood what this was all about, I found it hard to ask anyone to take over for a night. I felt guilty about taking any time to myself. I couldn't bear not responding instantly to any demand the children made. I felt guilty because they didn't have two parents. It was only when I began to make room for myself and my own

needs that I began to be a more effective parent. I was so drained before that I found I had nothing to give.

Caring for yourself physically, spiritually, and emotionally is a way of ensuring your ability to be able to meet the heavy demands that are on you.

Indeed, some parents become so depleted and so filled with bitterness that they begin to feel that their own needs are all that count. In these cases children can be thrust onto their own resources so much that they develop insecurity from the rejection they feel. One very sad young man told us:

> I get tired of eating dinner alone. My mom goes out almost every night. She leaves me a TV dinner, and I watch television and eat alone. It's fun sometimes not to have to follow rules. But I feel as if Mom really wishes she didn't have me to worry about; then she could live her life like she wants to.

Of course we're not suggesting that the parents' needs are *more* important than those of the children. In fact, children are entitled to adequate parenting. The point is that to be an adequate parent you need to take care of yourself. That means having adult friends, having some time alone, and having time for recreation—but all in accordance with the necessary time you must spend with your children.

The other side of the coin is that children should not be so protected, so hovered over that they never learn to care for themselves. We have to start very early in the life of children helping them to grow out of their need for us. This is a very difficult task for every parent, but even more so for the single parent who becomes dependent on the children to supply all of the parent's needs for love.

Healthy child development is a reflection of parents who find room for themselves, find meaning and freedom, and are in a position to bring a framework of discipline, fairness, and love into the parenting. Often parents in two-parent families have never had the occasion to work through the mature adult parenting stance that is forced on the strong single parent.

What keeps single parents from achieving this kind of healthy, mature parenting stance? Why are there so many who have not been able to work through the panic stage into an adult acceptance of what has happened and to become able to focus on the tasks at hand? Is it some blockage from within the parent that holds him or her back? Is it guilt over what has befallen the children? Is it a lack of self-worth that springs up from rejection or abandonment? Or is it the way society reacts to the separation and the situation confronting the parent and the children? Is it the gradual withdrawal of old friends, the self-conscious "protection" in speech and action on the part of old friends? Or is it just the hard facts of economics, health, energy, and time that depletes one?

Almost never is it just one of these things, but the way you feel about yourself is reinforced or negated by the way people act and by the problems you face.

The substance of "finding room" for the self has to do with self-worth in the context of what is happening in the environment around you. There are appropriate and inappropriate ways of engaging the environmental factors. These ways may very well be rooted in the long development from childhood of ways you have coped with stress, disappointment, and problems. Stresses in the environment may underscore the tendencies toward defeat and self-negation, and these inner feelings in turn may skew the ways in which one responds.

I feel I'm no good; people act as if I'm no good; therefore, I'm no good.

Dealing with Stress

Divorce is one of the most stress-producing events that can occur in the life of an individual. The separation itself and the unhappiness it brings are hard enough, but there are other stress-producing changes that accompany the separation both for the parents and for the children:

- The family may have to move from the home in order to make a property settlement.
- The financial pressures may increase dramatically in order to maintain two homes.
- The children may have to adjust to their parents' new relationships or to stepparents.
- The custodial parent may have to find employment instead of staying at home.

- Many changes in schedules may be necessary to allow for visitation.
- Children may have to spend more time alone or in a child-care arrangement.

The list could go on and on. The point is that there is an enormous amount of stress that occurs during the separation and divorce, and measures must be taken to deal with it. Eating a balanced diet and getting plenty of rest are a good idea at any time, but they become especially important now. In addition, some kind of vigorous exercise will go a long way to discharge some of the tension you are having. The same is true for the children, and this may be a time for the whole family to look for a way to get into a program of exercise.

There are opportunities in every community to participate in growth seminars and workshops. It may help you to find a class in assertiveness training, in enhancing your self-esteem, or even in how to reduce stress. Your adult evening school may offer these kinds of programs. Faith renewal classes in your church may speak to your need.

Let's take a look at the typical ways that single parents handle periods of stress. We have to remember that fears and anxieties rise up where there is frustration or an overload of seemingly impossible demands on time and energy. How do people handle these?

Some people go numb, and with an air of fatalism simply flow with the events, feeling that there is no use fighting it any longer.

I realized I couldn't handle what was going on, and I decided that it was "in the cards" for me to fail at parenting as well as everything else that I had tried. So I said to myself, "Why fight it?" What I could do, I did. What I couldn't do, I shrugged off with the thought that no one could blame me for not doing what I couldn't do. If my children suffered, so did I. They are young and probably can come out of it. As for me, I decided there wasn't much for me anyhow. So I let things go—I let everything go— the house, my appearance, any enjoyment for myself, friendships, everything. The word "numb" best describes it. My whole life felt numb.

This reaction to stress represents an advanced form of withdrawal from the conflict. The person is sinking into depression, and unless something or someone comes along to help, the withdrawal will continue. This person could benefit from professional care. While the depression may be brief and in time might cure itself, chances are that attention at this time would speed up the recovery and perhaps prevent a more serious form of depression.

Other persons take a different path in the face of stressful events. One of the reactions commonly seen is a pattern of hostility that can be triggered by almost anything that seems to go wrong: angry tirades to the teacher when the report card shows a near-failing grade, angry confrontations with the neighbors when a child reports being "picked on" in the school bus, accusations and threats hurled at the school counselor who intimates that Johnny might have been implicated in a loss of property at school, a severance of all relationship with the grandparents who suggest a better way of discipline.

Instinctively we gather our forces to act when we are threatened. It's like our bodily reaction when there is a sudden threat to us. In response to a loud noise or a threatening presence, adrenalin is pumped into our systems. Our hearts pound, our pulse is rapid, and we breathe rapidly. We feel the urge to do something—to run, if nothing more. Socially and relationally we gather our forces and feel the urge to do something, to strike back. There are always appropriate and inappropriate responses, and there is always the danger of trying to suppress the responses as if nothing had happened.

There are those who head into disastrous courses of escape: they begin to abuse alcohol or other drugs; they jump into another relationship immediately, sometimes with disastrous consequences; they may become dependent on parents and allow the parents to take over their job; or in some rare cases they may actually abandon their children.

Children have amazing defenses which enable them to survive this kind of emotional roller-coaster behavior in their parents. Very often a child making trouble in school is a child who is crying out for help for the whole family. If he or she is bad enough, then someone will pay attention and perhaps help the family.

Another way children react is to take over the reins themselves. Even young children can sometimes rally the family into a functioning unit when a parent lets down. This responsibility probably won't do any harm for a brief period of time. Most of us have to call on our children for help occasionally. But if the child has to become the parent on a permanent basis, he or she is being robbed of childhood and will have to make up those years at a later time.

We're sure that most people reading this book do not want to follow any of the patterns we have described. There are some things you can do to avoid these behaviors, and that's what we mean by finding "standing room" for yourself.

1. Feel entitled to ask for help whenever events seem to be overwhelming you. Help is available from many sources. Family and friends want to help. If you are making a genuine effort for yourself, so that you are not simply becoming dependent, then reach out and tell them that you are desperate. They will respond.

2. When the children are away visiting their other parent, take advantage of that time to pamper yourself. If you can't afford to get away, at least get some simple relaxation and rest.

3. Keep a journal of what is happening to you. You will find that you can see your progress week-by-week as you check back through the journal, and this will encourage you to go on.

4. Insist that the children do their part in assuming appropriate responsibilities in the house. All but the youngest children can do something, and it is as important to their self-esteem as to your own that they participate.

5. If you can't afford to belong to an exercise club, get in the habit of vigorous walking or running if your doctor approves. This activity costs nothing, but it is very useful in relieving stress.

6. Ask your physician if there are any vitamin supplements that would help you at this time.

7. Don't hesitate to ask for professional help when you need it. There's nothing wrong with admitting that you can't handle the situation.

8. Explore your own religious faith and seek God's help in

the midst of the circumstances surrounding you.

The most important thing you can do for your children is to make sure that you are taking care of yourself. You are their rock, you are the teacher of your children, and you can teach them that they can trust you to be there for them, to be available to them when they need you. You must find ways to have confidence in yourself in order for them to live confidently, joyously, and productively. Have faith in yourself and in God and discover new ways to restore your spirit.

9

Dating and the Children

For everything there is a season, and a time for every matter under heaven:

a time to be born, and a time to die;
a time to plant, and a time to pluck up what is planted;
a time to kill, and a time to heal;
a time to break down, and a time to build up;
a time to weep, and a time to laugh;
a time to mourn, and a time to dance;
a time to cast away stones, and a time to gather stones together;
a time to embrace, and a time to refrain from embracing;
a time to seek, and a time to lose;
a time to keep, and a time to cast away;
a time to rend, and a time to sew;
a time to keep silence, and a time to speak;
a time to love, and a time to hate;
a time for war, and a time for peace.

—Ecclesiastes 3:1-8

In spite of firm resolutions to the contrary, most healthy divorced persons come to a time when they are willing to recognize that they need adult companionship, that they need to be loved, and that they still have the capacity to love. Their reluctance to think about dating or remarrying stems from their grief over the broken relationship, deep disappointment in marriage, feelings of inadequacy, fears of repeated failure, and an inability to let go of the former relationship. Also they worry about the effects on their children. Each of these feelings is real. All of them need to be dealt with, and divorced persons probably are not ready for other relationships until they have done so.

A Time to Weep

Our culture has always been more clear about the need for mourning the death of a loved one than about mourning the loss of a loved one through divorce. In former times there was a generally accepted period, usually a year, when the grieving widow was expected to refrain from social engagements or relationships with other partners. We even had symbols of mourning, a black armband, for example, which signified the period of grief.

Broken relationships, whatever the cause, require a time for healing, a period during which the persons involved can let themselves weep, hurt, and finally come through the pain. We have people asking us, "How long does the period of grief last?" Nobody can answer that question for you or for your children. Sometimes the grief period begins long before the marriage ends, just as in a prolonged illness the persons close to a dying loved one gradually accept the inevitability of approaching death. By the time of the actual death, part of the grieving is done, and much of the pain of separation has been endured. In this situation, a person learns to let go a little at a time, and the same is true in divorce. In those cases, the period of grief is usually shorter than when the realization comes suddenly and without warning. But if, long after the divorce or separation, you find that you or your children still cry at the mention of the absent spouse, then it is time for you to seek some help to understand your feelings. This letting go doesn't mean, of course, that you won't continue to have occasional pangs of emotional distress when something reminds you of happy times you spent together with the former mate, or that you won't from time to time wish that you could recapture those good times you spent together. That is to be expected. Your children will experience those same feelings, and you should encourage them to talk about their happy memories. But the Scripture informs us that there is also a time to laugh, and you will have to help your children learn to laugh again and to do so without feeling guilty about it. This happens most easily when you convince yourself that the time for weeping is over and that the time for moving on has come.

A Time to Sew

You've been wounded. Your hopes and dreams about "forever after" have been shattered, and the disappointment that you feel and the fear of repeating your failure are so overwhelming that you are reluctant to risk trying again. Still, at those moments of high emotion when you experience something beautiful or something sad, you long for someone to share with you those feelings. Many people have expressed to us their mixed emotions. They feel very lonely and yet they are afraid of being hurt; they want to live a more "normal" social life in what they perceive as a couples' world, but they worry about repeating their past failure.

Obviously if you have not used this time of mourning and adjustment to examine closely what happened to your marriage and what part you had in its failure, if you leap into another marriage without careful thought and adequate preparation, if you allow yourself to seek a mate with the same inadequacies of your former one, and if you marry for financial security only, you are at a high risk of repeating the pattern. There's no guarantee that any marriage will work, but there are ways to lessen the risk.

The first thing you must do before you allow yourself to become involved in another relationship is to finish the business of ending your relationship with the former spouse. When the grieving is over, when you have truly let go of any hope of recapturing that relationship, when your anger has subsided enough (continuing to battle the former spouse is a sure sign that you are *not* through), then the time has come for you to face yourself and your own needs by trying to understand what happened. This self-examination may require some third-party help so that you don't end up still blaming the other person for it all, or feeling guilty and blaming yourself. Placing blame is not the goal of this kind of examination; understanding is.

Through this kind of process will come growth. Although growth is usually painful, you may be able to see that even out of failure has come insight and strength. When that happens, you are much better prepared to risk again. Surely there is risk involved, but there is no relationship without risk.

On the other hand, you may decide that because of religious beliefs or because you enjoy the freedom of being single, you don't want to be married again. You don't have to get married, but most of us enjoy male/female relationships if for no other reason than companionship. You need to understand what it is you are looking for when you enter the social world of singleness.

Another concern is how you choose your companions. The singles world is loaded with exploiters, both male and female. Because you are naive to that very different world, because you are scared, and because you want to succeed, you are vulnerable. Read everything you can, talk with others who are single and have more experience than you, and then step cautiously. Know what it is you want, and don't accept anything less. Be aware of the effects on your children when you date and insist that the persons you date take the children's needs into consideration. If they cannot understand your concerns, they are not good company for you in the long run, anyhow. It may be your time to dance, but you may want to start with the Virginia Reel before you try break dancing!

A Time to Embrace, or a Time to Refrain

I felt like a fool. There I was a middle-aged woman of forty-two with two teenage daughters helping me to get ready for a date. I was so nervous I could hardly make up my mind what I would wear. At first the girls were excited, but as the time approached for my date to arrive, they began anxiously questioning me about where I was going and when I would come home.

This situation is not an unusual one. The mother in this case was a very attractive woman, and her two teenage daughters were not particularly good looking and had not as yet started to date. They later became resentful of the fact that their mother's social life was so much better than their own. They worried about their mother's safety and about her possible intimate relationship with the men she was seeing.

The mother's anxiety about the date was also similar to that of many others. She worried about how she looked, what she would talk about, and how she would react if the man made demands on her. In effect, she was feeling as if she were living her adolescent years all over again, and she was not sure that she was up to it.

We believe that parents who are dating should begin to do so without exposing the children to the dates. It is better for them, as long as the relationship is casual, for you to meet the companion outside the home. If the relationship becomes more serious, and you feel that it may evolve into a long-term relationship, then it would be appropriate for you to have the children meet the person. Handling your social relationships in this way avoids the roller coaster of emotions that is sometimes brought on by multiple short-term acquaintances. You will of course let the children know that you are going out with someone, and you should let them know where you are going and what time they can expect you home, just as you would expect your children to inform you about their social life. *Don't lie to them* and expect that they will be truthful with you. You are entitled to have companionship, both male and female, and you need not apologize about it. Before you ever start to date, sit down with your children and tell them you are thinking about it because you need companionship. Let them know that you respect their need for friends and will do all you can to see that their friendships are encouraged; thus you can expect they will do the same for you. Assure them that they will be the first to know if a relationship develops into something serious, but at the beginning you are seeking only to have someone share some good times.

It is very difficult for children to see their parents embracing an opposite-sex adult. Not only does it raise the loyalty issue for them (I wish Mommy were hugging and kissing Daddy instead of this other man), but it also feels to them that if you are going to give your love to this other person there will be less for them. We heard one very sensitive man tell his children: "Love is not like a pie where the more pieces you cut the less there is for everyone. Rather love is like a balloon, and the more love you get, the bigger is your ability to love." He helped his children to understand that he needed more love so he would have more love to give them.

You will need to keep your embracing within bounds at the beginning while you are in sight of the children. They don't have to be very old before they read affectionate touching as indicating that you are more intimate out of their sight and hearing. A young man said to us:

> They make me sick. They aren't together two minutes before he is all over her. He kisses her on the mouth, the neck, the ear, and they look at each other like some cheap movie. I hate it!

Even in two-parent families small children are apt to feel envious of their parents embracing, as they feel shut out of the love. How many times have you seen a two- or three-year-old try to get between his parents when they are kissing?

We are not saying that you should never embrace when your children are around. It would not be natural for you to be so restricted. But if the relationship is not a serious one, and if the children have not had time to get used to the idea, keep the touching to a minimum.

Many writers in this field give approval to having a partner spend the night or move in with the single parent if the relationship has reached a deep level. Even if we assume that there would never be any sexual intimacy within sight or hearing of the children, we have strong reservations about the live-in or overnight partner so long as children are in the house. How can you expect your children to give any credence to your pleas for their having sexual restraint when you are unwilling to do so? As an adult you are entitled to do whatever you wish with your sexuality, but our concern is for the double standard that you set for your children.

Single parents tell us that their young children often wait until they are ready to leave on a date to "act up." They get hysterical; they develop pains; they may even vomit. The parent is faced with a dilemma: Shall I go and leave my child in distress, or shall I tell the date that I can't go? It is difficult to make a blanket statement about what is right because sometimes these symptoms are real. It's not uncommon for families to report illnesses developing in their children at most inopportune moments. One way to handle the situation is to attend to the immediate symptoms, leave, and then telephone home within an hour to see if the problem has subsided. We assume that you would not leave your young children with other than competent help, and that you would have emergency telephone numbers available so that the sitter could call for help if necessary. You can usually determine whether the child is truly ill by checking for elevation of temperature and for other signs of serious illness. Also, you will, over a period of time, observe whether or not the child has a pattern of developing illness when you are going out. One mother confessed to us that she realized later that she had inadvertently set up her son to misbehave when her date was present by warning the child that he must "be good" while her boyfriend was present or else the boyfriend might leave. The child thus had a scenario for what to do to get rid of someone who was his rival for his mother's attention.

It's not unheard of for older children to come up with emergency situations also. Part of this behavior is to discourage you from going out, and sometimes it is to discourage the companion from wanting to date anyone whose family causes problems. Usually when children are faced with these possibilities, they will deny it. They may not even be conscious that they are engaging in unfair tactics. If you talk with them about it, many children are willing to examine their behavior and try to change.

In order for you to be able to handle these situations, you must be convinced in your own mind that it is right for you to have some time away from your children, and that it is up to you to decide when, where, and with whom you will go. Obviously you are going to make sure that you are available for at least the majority of the occasions when your children need you. If they have a school performance or a sports event in which they are participating, they have a right to expect that you will make every effort to be present. Their schedules have a way of limiting your own, and this is a reality you will have to accept if you expect to provide them with the security they deserve. Many times school events take place during the working day when it is impossible for a parent to be present. Children can accept this if there is a good reason, but not if it is a matter of your putting your pleasure ahead of your concern for them.

The other side of that reality is that you need time for play and relaxation with other adults if you are to have the resources to give of yourself to your children. Something has to go into the bank if you are to draw any interest. All parents find themselves better able to deal with the problems of parenthood if they have opportunities to get away occasionally. Children benefit by having a happier, more relaxed parent after these times of respite. Having a parent play the martyr is not in the children's best interest.

A Time to Gather

Not all of the opposite-sex close relationships you have will necessarily be preludes to marriage. We know many single parents who have formed close relationships with opposite-sex friends whom they did not plan to marry, but with whom they could have a good time and who enjoyed being with children. Jack and Barbara are such a pair. Jack is a widower with two children (aged twelve and ten), and Barbara is a divorcee with three young children (aged five, six, and eight). Both families liked the out-of-doors, but Barbara hesitated to go camping alone with her children. Jack's family enjoyed camping, had all the camping equipment, but somehow couldn't bring themselves to go after the death of his wife. Jack talked with his children about it, and they liked the idea of teaching Barbara's young family how to handle themselves in an outdoor setting. They now plan to camp together several times during good weather, and both families have benefited greatly from the experience. They take two tents on these outings, and Barbara sleeps in one tent with her children, Jack and his children in the other.

There are many rewards from this kind of arrangement: (1) Pooling resources makes it possible for both families to vacation with a minimum of expense. (2) It exposes the children to more relationships with the same-sex adult as their absent parent. These relationships are particularly important to Barbara and Jack because Barbara has no close male relatives, and Jack's relatives live many miles away. Thus the children lack role models. (3) Since the children all know that

Jack and Barbara are not romantically involved, they are free to have a nonthreatening relationship with an adult whom they have learned to admire and trust. (4) Jack's older children feel good about being "teachers" to Barbara's younger ones and thus have increased their self-esteem. (5) Both families are learning to live together with others, and this may be good preparation for the day when either Jack or Barbara decides to remarry.

A Time to Keep, A Time to Cast Away

Let's suppose that you have found someone you really like and have decided that it is time for the children to meet your friend. You bring the person home and find that without warning your children are suddenly hostile or greet the friend with stony silence. After several attempts to be friendly, you and your friend decide to abandon the meeting and he or she leaves. After you try again and again, and you become more and more anxious and are feeling angry about their behavior, you face the children and insist that they talk with you about why they have been so uncooperative.

If you find that they simply don't like the person, try to get them to be more specific. It is possible that they have discovered some basic flaw in the person which you have not seen and which you may realize is an important consideration if your relationship is to be successful. In this way their reaction may be beneficial.

On the other hand, it may be that the children had a preconceived bias against your friend or against anyone you might consider marrying. They may have made up their minds that they are not going to cooperate, either because they want to have your exclusive attention, or because they are expressing loyalty to your former spouse. If you believe this to be the case, then there is no reason for you to discontinue your relationship. It is simply not appropriate for your children to be choosing your companions. Certainly, unless they can be helped to accept the intended mate, your marriage is going to have some difficult days. Sometimes engaging the family in counseling with the intended can be useful both in helping to uncover the hidden agenda and in bringing about some solutions to the problems.

Keep your companion if the problem is with the children, or

resolve to "cast him or her away" if the problem is with the companion and he or she is unwilling to address the problem.

A Time to Love

This may truly be a time for you to learn to love again, a time to let yourself live again. Having someone who is interested in you and who finds you fun to be with will make so much difference in your ability to face the problems that are inevitable in parenting. It helps you to regain some of your lost self-esteem—"I am lovable" is a feeling that brings great joy to any person of any age. We would encourage you to risk letting that happen to you when the time comes even if the risk you take is an informed risk. A time of hating takes a tremendous toll; when the season is right for loving, allow that season to bring a greening and blossoming to your life.

10

If You Marry Again

Your decision to marry for a second or third time is an adult decision. It is not one that should be handed over to the children. Even in cases where the children are fond of the intended spouse, they are caught in a loyalty bind: How can I be loyal to my own parent and at the same time have a loving relationship with my parent's new spouse? Obviously a caring parent is going to take the children into consideration in making a decision to remarry. You certainly would not deliberately choose someone who did not care for your children, or whom you felt would not be a good parent for them. But taking them into consideration and allowing them to make the decision for you are two different matters. Just as the decision to separate is an adult decision, so is the decision to remarry.

One of the questions you should ask yourself in making that decision is whether or not you have allowed the children to get to know the intended spouse. Have you seen them together enough to know how well they relate to each other? Is the prospective husband or wife sensitive to the needs and fears of the children? Is he or she able to handle the children's times of poor behavior as well as their times of good behavior?

Another question that could help you in making your decision is how does my prospective spouse treat his or her own children? Does he or she make a genuine effort to continue to be a responsible parent? Even when the former spouse of your prospective mate has made visitation very difficult, you will want to know what steps he or she has taken to try to overcome the difficulties. This picture will tell you a great deal about the parenting potential of your intended. All kinds of excuses are used for abandoning children: "I decided that it would be better for the children if they never saw me." "I just got tired of the battle and gave up." "My former husband has turned the children against me, and I just decided that it wasn't worth the effort. If they don't want to see me, I don't want to see them." In addition to displaying insensitivity, this parent is giving a strong message to you—he or she is unable to express the pain which this kind of separation produces and probably has trouble expressing feelings about other things as well.

In almost all cases the parent who has abandoned his or her own children finds it very difficult to give to the children who are not his or hers. Deep inside will be the grinding knowledge that those other children whom he or she has not been able to parent are out there somewhere. This situation is a set-up for difficulties between the person and a new spouse whose children will be making claims for themselves.

Who Will Be the Parent?

Many second marriages start off with the partners deciding that each of them will be in charge of his or her own children. That is, the husband will make the rules for the children he had before the marriage, and the wife will make the rules for hers. This kind of arrangement is a reminder of the phrase, "an accident looking for a place to happen." We've heard sad stories over and over. Here is Charles's story:

I went out last night and left the kids home with Mary. They are both teenagers and mouthy at times, but usually I can handle them when I'm there. Mary was right in telling them to turn down their radios, which were blasting her out of the house, but they refused to pay any attention to her. One said, "Hey, you can't tell me what to do! Dad told us we were allowed to play our radios until bedtime, and that's what we're doing. You're not our mother."

When I got home, Mary was off the wall. She hit me with it the minute I opened the door. "Those kids of yours are driving me crazy. . . . I think it's going to be them or me. Make your choice."

Essentially, Charles and Mary had a good marriage. They had fun together, their sex life was good, they had lots of friends, and they had truly let go of their former relationships and had worked through their own part in their divorces. They shared many of the same values, and they had long-term goals for themselves and their families, but they had not found a satisfactory way to parent their children under the new circumstances. What they had failed to realize was that nobody should be given the role of parent without being allowed to have the responsibility for parenting.

Mary had two children of her own, but they were much younger than Charles's children. She had not had the experience to help her understand the teenager. In addition, she was put in the position of helplessness when it came to making rules. Her style of parenting was much more strict than that of Charles, but they both had the same goals. If they had been careful to work out a code of behavior that was acceptable to both of them, had they informed all of the children of that code, and if they had been able to agree that when one was absent, the other was in charge, the situation would have been much easier to handle. Children will push adults as far as they can, and they are eternally testing to see if they can find a soft spot in the armor. Charles and Mary were able to see this after a while and work out some agreement, as Charles described it:

> We had a meeting with all of the kids, and we told them that there was going to be a new approach to discipline in the house. We agreed that I could not be Mary's kids' father, and she could not be my kids' mother, but that we could both be parents to all of the kids. We expected that when one was absent, the other was in charge, and the kids were expected to treat that parent with respect and to carry out the rules. We agreed that there would be a regular family meeting where any complaints could be

registered and dealt with fairly. We were amazed at how well all this was received. I know the war isn't over, but I think we're in a much better position now.

There's nothing wrong with two people having different styles of parenting, provided they are within the realm of reason. Suppose that one parent is more strict than the other. Each can help to temper the other's approach and sometimes prevent the decision from being either too hard or too soft. The important thing is for each parent to respect the other and for them to be able to negotiate a style of parenting that is acceptable to both. These kinds of issues need to be explored before the marriage takes place. Both of you probably have some experience at parenting, and so you are better prepared to state how you see the task being carried out. This was not true in the first marriage in all likelihood. Neither you nor your first spouse may have been parents before the marriage.

Who's in Charge?

In some of our parenting classes we like to have the participants role-play familiar family situations. It is always interesting to see who takes charge in these little vignettes. Given the task of planning a family vacation, we often see one of the adults who is playing a child take complete charge. The person will use every trick in the book to manipulate the situation so that the child gets the rest of the family to agree to the child's will. Most of the time the "adults" will not even notice that they are being manipulated, that their own needs or other family members' needs are not being heard. The family will agree to a vacation far beyond their means just to end the battle. The role play helps the participants and the audience to look at the dynamics of the situation and decide what has actually taken place.

Children need to be heard, their wishes need to be taken into account in family decisions, but ultimately the decision must be made by the adult or adults in the family. It is much healthier for the child to be secure in the knowledge that someone is in charge. The position need not be as extreme as a friend of ours put it, "I believe in democracy in the family so long as everyone understands who's king!"

A Question of Turf

When we do premarital counseling with a couple who are marrying for the second time, we encourage them to think carefully about where they are going to live. Not everyone has a choice in this, of course, because the economics of the situation will sometimes dictate where you will live. But let's suppose that you both own property, that your children are old enough, and you are far enough away from the divorce to allow their adjustment; then you may want to think through all of the possibilities in a little different light. It is very hard sometimes for children to adjust to having someone else come onto their "turf" and take over a role they would prefer to have filled by their mother or father. "That's not the way my mother did it," or "This isn't your house," are the familiar phrases. As a matter of fact this matter of ownership is very often a problem for the adults who remarry. We have heard some bizarre stories about the way a husband or wife bristles at the change in routines, or even the rearrangement of furniture.

For these reasons you may want to think about liquidating both your present properties and investing in a new place so that neither of you has a lot of memories, both good and bad, tied up in the place where you choose to live.

When the decision is that you will live in one or the other's present home—whether rented, owned, or even an apartment— you will want to think about ways that you can help the person moving in to feel some ownership of the home. Bringing some familiar things from their former home—something familiar like their old mantle clock whose chimes sound so good—can provide meaning and security to the children while enriching the home. Even a little attention in regard to the furnishings and the way things are arranged can give satisfaction and a feeling of security or belonging.

Adjusting to the New Family

Where there are different habits of long standing, negotiated changes are in order. It may be the time of the dinner hour— one is used to an early dinner, the other to a later time. You might decide to eat early on week nights and later on weekends. With thought beforehand, most of the accustomed routines can be accommodated. Children can benefit from seeing that everyone's desires are taken into account. It's good for them to bend also. Insecure children can seem very inflexible in regard to patterns of home life. Learning that you insist on their treating your new spouse with respect and cooperation in working out new routines about the household can give the children a valuable lesson in relationships.

Cooperation and respect are, of course, a two-way street. The newcomer to the family must be aware of the children's fears and apprehensions, as well as their feelings of split loyalties. You have to earn the right to be a parent in this situation. The only thing these children owe you at the beginning is respect because you are their parent's spouse. As you demonstrate your trustability and availability to them, you will earn their allegiance to yourself. Because you are older and more able to understand what is going on, you may have to give more than you receive for a while. But if they find that you are firm but fair, if they discover that they can trust you with their feelings, there will come a time when you can truly be friends, and you can add a great deal to each other's lives.

New Spouse Who Has No Children

We once spent time with a couple who were about to be married who felt that they had worked through all of the possible problems. They had been dating for a few months, and they believed in that time they had come to know each other completely. They said that they had no money problems. They stated that their sex life was great. They had separate interests, and she said that she didn't mind that he was a workaholic. They were going to live in a new house and had compromised on the furnishings—he liked antiques and she liked contemporary, so they had compromised on "Chinese modern". Everything was all neatly tied-up with a ribbon. It seemed just a little too easy. We were seeing them because they had gone to a clergyman requesting a marriage date immediately and he had been very hesitant, insisting that they engage in premarital counseling before he would marry them. So they had come to us under duress, which is hardly the best motivation for counseling.

Jenny had been formerly married for twenty years and had

a son (fourteen) and a daughter (seventeen), both living at home. Now divorced, their father had moved to another state and the children didn't even want to see him, nor apparently did he want to see them. Jeff was in his mid-forties, a successful businessman, who still lived at home with his parents. He insisted that he lived an entirely independent life; so there was no problem with his family. When we raised a question about the children, there was finally a little wavering on Jeff's part about the perfection of their relationship.

The only problem we have, which of course we can handle, is that she isn't as strict with the children as I think she should be. She waits on them hand and foot; they don't lift a finger to do anything. I think it has to be a cooperative venture, this living together. I don't think it would be fair for me to sit reading a newspaper while my wife did all the cooking and cleaning up, and I don't think it should be that way for the children, either. They aren't little; they're adults. She has been trying so hard to make up to them the fact that they haven't had a father that she has spoiled them rotten. She's going to talk to them, however, and let them know that the rules are going to be changed.

This couple is headed for trouble. In spite of the fact that the children profess their approval of the marriage, can you imagine how well they will receive the news that their long-established way of life will change to the point of their having to take a full share of responsibility in the house? Even if they are willing to go along with the plan, their resentment toward Jeff is bound to be great. Jenny is going to be caught in the middle between her new husband and her children, and she will undoubtedly begin to feel resentful toward Jeff. The fact that Jeff has been living with his family of origin for forty-three years will have a lot to do with the way he is able to fit into this new family. It's hard to imagine that he has not been pampered by his parents or that he has not developed a strong feeling of responsibility for them. Learning to live with young adults after years of living with older adults will present some inevitable problems which this couple is not facing with any reality.

The transition period for a stepparent may be much easier

or much more difficult with older children. Sometimes older children are anxious to have their parents remarry, for they feel strongly the responsibility for taking care of their parent. It's a relief to these older children to have someone else willing to take over the job. On the other hand, if there has been a great deal of hostility toward a parent who has left, then remarriage can cause the focus of that hostility to be shifted to the new stepparent.

Children, wishing their parents to be together no matter what, will try in every way possible to bring those parents back together, just as they will try everything possible to break up new alliances. It is important for you and your new mate to be aware of these kinds of shenanigans and be prepared to meet them together. These behavior patterns are neither abnormal nor unusual. They are the norm rather than the exception. If your resolve is firm, you won't be nearly as vulnerable. The temptation is to feel sorry for the child and to give yourself a guilt trip all over again. You should be convinced *before you marry* that you are finished with the first marriage, and that this new one is right for you and in the long run for your children.

Examining the Reason for Marriage

We have heard many very sad people report that they decided to enter a second marriage because they needed a father or a mother for their children. Hardly anyone would disagree that it is better for children to grow up in a household with two parents, and it is certainly easier to have someone with whom you can share the load. But providing a parent for your children should not be the primary reason for marriage. You should have learned by now that marriage is pretty serious stuff, and divorce courts are full of people who will say that they got married for the wrong reasons. One person quipped that marriage is a kind of Russian roulette, and the only ones that make it are just lucky because most people enter marriage when they are too young to have any idea of what they will face in the years to come. We ought to get smarter as we get older, but sadly, few of us do. We believe that it would not be a bad idea for all couples considering marriage to spend some serious time in counseling, examining their family legacy of relationship, their expectations of each other in the marriage, and learning skills for handling the stressful situations that will inevitably arise. For the second and subsequent marriages, where there are children involved, this would include an examination of parenting styles and expectations. With a competent counselor the time and effort would be a wise investment.

Financial Considerations

We are strong advocates of a prenuptial agreement. This agreement is a legal contract executed before the marriage which can safeguard any assets the individuals may have from inclusion in a community property settlement. In some cases both parties to a marriage elect to set aside whatever assets each of them brings to the marriage for future distribution to their own children. Sometimes only a portion of the holdings is included, depending on the circumstances. Children, even very young children, are concerned about what is going to happen to their inheritance, and this concern can become one reason why children are so resistant to the marriage. If, when you let them know you are planning to remarry, you can reassure them about their future inheritance, it will relieve some of their anxiety—"That was my father's money, and she has no right to give it to someone else."

This approach may seem mercenary to you, and of course it is up to you to decide what you will do with your assets, but the inheritance, no matter how small, may be the only remnant the children have of their life together with their mother and father.

Prenuptial agreements are not chiseled in stone. After the marriage has survived a long time, you can decide to tear up the agreement. But anyone who has gone through a divorce is painfully aware of the difficulties encountered in property settlement. Remember, prenuptial agreements can provide for adequate financial support if the marriage ends in divorce. Housing can be provided for a surviving spouse until his or her death, allowing the spouse to live in a house which will later become the property of the dead spouse's children. These agreements can be varied in so many ways, and a competent attorney will help you and your prospective mate to decide what you want to do.

Unequal Treatment of Children

A complaint heard very often among the children of a second marriage is that of having a stereotypical "wicked stepmother or stepfather." And sometimes, unfortunately, it is true. Let's suppose that the wife's children live with her, and the husband's children come for weekend visits. The wife is fed up with the demands of her husband's former wife, with the amount of support he is paying, and with the fact that every weekend is preempted from any social life for her and her husband because of his children's visit. Her anger at her husband, which she finds hard to voice, may get played out against his children. She resists his efforts to do things with his children, and she treats them differently from her own, offering her own children privileges and favors that she refuses to give to his children. She bad-mouths their mother and tries to extract information from them about such matters as the amount of money the mother makes. Is it any wonder if the children end up feeling that she is a witch?

This kind of retributive behavior on the part of a stepparent leads down a thorny path. It is a sure way to cause her husband to withdraw from her, because he is certain to feel caught in a trap. His need for quality time with his children is great. He has only a short time to express all of his pent-up feelings for his children, and they for him, and he will not long tolerate his wife's intolerance if he has any spunk at all.

The other side is that the spouse whose children are visiting must be aware of the disruption their visits cause to the household and recognize the sacrifices that are required on the part of the whole family in order to make the visits work. He or she must be willing to make sure that all that can be done to ease the pressure is done, and that the spouse's willingness to make the visits pleasant is acknowledged.

The problems of visitation are inescapable. Just when you think you have one facet worked out, there will be another. It takes tremendous patience and continuing determination to negotiate solutions to the problems. It can be done, no matter how difficult, provided both spouses are willing to focus on the children's needs and at the same time recognize that they themselves have to support each other through the more involved situations.

The Wedding

We have lots of reservations about the participation of children in their parents' weddings to new mates. Sometimes it works out fine. Sometimes the children are thrilled to get all dressed up and be the center of a lot of attention. For other children, there is so much emotion for them to handle, so many mixed feelings, that you will want to think carefully about what you ask of them. For example, a ten-year-old who "knows" that his father is still in love with his mother may be holding on to a secret wish that somehow a miracle will happen and they will get back together. The wedding represents an end to that dream. In some ways the event may help him to stop fantasizing. In other ways he feels so disloyal to his mother (or father) that he will be torn apart with guilt if he enjoys the day and somehow helps to make the wedding happen by participating. Make sure you think about the wedding from your child's point of view and discuss it with the child openly, helping him or her to voice the things about it that may be hard to say.

If you can (that is, if your relationship with your former spouse will permit it), be sure that your former spouse knows about the forthcoming wedding, knows the part the children will have in the ceremony, and has an opportunity to help the children handle their feelings. Jane, a former client of ours, described her own experience.

Fred and I had never been able to talk to each other without fighting, and we had reached the point where we hardly spoke to each other at all. He would come and pick up Emily and Jeanne (aged six and eight) without my ever having to see him. He'd bring them back and not even get out of the car. Our arrangement was that he had the girls every other weekend from Friday after school until after dinner on Sunday night.

One weekend, with no hint of anything special going on, the girls came running into the house on Sunday night dressed in beautiful new outfits and so excited. They had brought home a very special gift for me—it turned out to be the bride's bouquet of Fred's new wife. The girls had participated in the wedding wearing new outfits purchased on Saturday for the Sunday wedding. Neither they nor I had any idea that there was to be a wedding or that the girls would be involved. Can you imagine the shock I felt and the fury that engulfed me when those little girls handed me that bouquet? I don't think I cared that he was married; I was simply overcome by his insensitivity. I'm sure Emily and Jeanne will never forget the look on my face.

This case is extreme, of course, but it helps to illustrate the need to avoid unnecessary problems for your children.

11

Go for It!

Watching the 1984 Olympics, we heard over and over the various team members encouraging each other to win with the phrase "Go for it!" They meant, of course, that the athletes should let out all the stops, take the risks, and exert their greatest energy to win. Sometimes they won and sometimes they lost, but you had the feeling that they were all reaching for the gold.

This book has dealt mostly with the problems of divorce, and of necessity it has been a serious, sometimes somber discussion. We want it to be more than that. The single parents we work with have inspired us. They have shown us courage, resilience, and determination; they have astounded us with their ability to change; they have reached out in the most generous way to be of help to others.

We know that if you can catch a glimpse of the hope that has driven these others to step bravely forward, it will encourage you to do the same. You must take a look at the progress you are making already—you have learned to do things you never thought you could do, you have somehow been coping with some tough problems, and you are alive, perhaps "bent but not broken." Take the time to assess how far you have come already, and it will help you to continue your progress.

We ask you to take a leap of faith into the future. Believe that time will help to heal your pain; believe that there is a better tomorrow; believe that you are fully capable of raising those precious children and supporting them as they become healthy, well-adjusted members of society. Touch them a lot—hugs and kisses and stroking are good for both of you. Play with them, and run away to play with other adults sometimes.

We know a terrific woman whom we'll call Candy. She has five children, the oldest of whom is afflicted with Down's syndrome. Candy is raising her children alone and doing such a good job of it that she has been an inspiration to all of us. She works part time in an office every day, and she has had to organize her schedule so that she can spend time with her children, participate in their activities (two of them are in Little League baseball), and do the shopping and all of the household chores. She does all of those things and at the same time is able to do some things for herself. She bowls regularly and goes out with friends when she can arrange it. She has a great sense of humor and is fun to be around. Everyone around Candy feels her strength and her buoyant spirit and respects her for her devotion to her children.

Candy feels that there are some real advantages to being single. She got tired of being in the "you poor things" group at her church because she simply doesn't feel that way about her situation. She enjoys the freedom of being single—she can stay up half the night reading a book if she wants to (though of course she seldom has the energy to do so); she can take her kids and go somewhere for a day or two without having to coddle her husband into going. She doesn't have to worry about her husband's alcoholism, and she doesn't have to hassle about money. She doesn't have as much as when she was married, but at least she doesn't have to fight about it anymore. "I could sit around and feel sorry for myself," she says, "but what good would that do? I'm not willing to waste my time like that." Candy could probably marry again if she chose to, but she's satisfied right now to enjoy her children and let the future take care of itself.

We think that you too can be a Candy. You can stop looking

back and re-experiencing all the tears, the sorrows, the bitterness and begin to look to the future. The greatest thing about such an attitude is that it is contagious. You will give your children a message that there is hope, security, love, and joy in the future for them and for you.

Take some risks. We're not talking about jumping off a cliff and hoping you will land safely. The risks must be informed risks, but deciding to reach out for love again, determining that you will laugh again, and in every way you can, starting to rebuild relationships that will be supportive and caring—these are the risks that you can and must take.

You are the real expert on your family. Nobody else knows your family as well as you do, and no one else can do a better job of raising your children than you.

Our message to you is a loud and vigorous challenge: **Go for it!**

Questions for Thought and/or Discussion

Chapter 1: The Marriage Is Over

1. We hear people say, "We are staying together only for the sake of the kids." If the marriage relationship is permanently broken, list the values, in respect to the children, of the parents staying together until the children grow up, or of the parents separating.

2. If children learn how to relate to other people by what happens in the home, what important things can the children learn when their father and mother separate?

3. Some separated men and women say, "I can't bear to tell my friends and my family, much less to ask for their help." What is appropriate and what is inappropriate in seeking help from family and friends?

4. "I never talk to my children about the divorce; it is past and done with." What is right and what is wrong with that statement?

5. "I feel so sorry for my kids; now they have no chance for a normal life." How do you respond to that?

Chapter 2: Telling the Children

1. A woman said to the counselors, "Don't mention 'divorce' in the hearing distance of the children; I don't want them to know about it." In what ways do children pick up knowledge about parental discord? What is the basis of the fear children have of possible divorce?

2. Why is it important for separating parents to tell the children together?

3. When one parent refuses to talk to the children, what are the dangers of making up "excuses" to the children or of assailing and putting down the parent?

4. Should it be left up to the children to cast the deciding vote on whether or not to separate? on what the living arrangements will be?

5. Why is it important for the children that the teachers at school know of the separation? that the extended family members know?

Chapter 3: Decisions, Decisions

1. What is the most important factor to consider when deciding which parent is to have custody?

2. Why is it important to keep siblings together in custody arrangements when it is possible?

3. A father said, "Because I love my children, I want to go away so they will never see me again and will forget me." Why is it important for children to have access to both parents? Do you agree with the tendency of judges to make decisions about custody in terms of the parents' ability to care for the children *and* the likelihood of having access to both parents?

4. What value is there in having the two parents agree on custody before the court decision?

5. Where there is a "friendly" agreement, why should there be any kind of formal or legal agreement?

6. What is wrong in encouraging children to skip visits with the absent parent if the child says, "I don't want to go"?

Chapter 4: Children in the Middle

1. What is the danger in harrassing the absent parent to visit the children? What negative impact may it have on the absent parent? on the custodial parent? on the children?

2. What does it mean that children may become "message carriers"? What is the difference between encouraging "message carrying" and showing interest in the experience of the children?

3. How can the custodial parent and the noncustodial parent reduce the competition for the affection of the children? How do children consciously or unconsciously take advantage of competitiveness between the parents? What harm does that do the child?

4. It is said that children never cease wishing their divorced parents were together (even if they strongly disapprove behaviors related to the separation); what are appropriate ways for the parents to react to such direct or indirect attitudes?

5. What does it mean for children to become "parentified"? Why is this damaging to the children?

6. Why do parents tend to overprotect the children after the separation? What negative effect does this have on the children?

Chapter 5: The Pain of It All

1. One mother said, "I don't ever let them (the children) know that I am hurting." What does the stoic denial of feelings teach the children? Is it really good for the children?

2. A father lectures the son on visiting days, "Don't act like a crybaby; be a man!" whenever the boy shows emotion about what has happened at school or on the playground. What are the positive and negative values being taught by this advice?

3. Sometimes children pretend nothing has happened. What is an appropriate way for parents to respond to this reaction?

4. What do you think children fear the most after parents are divorced?

5. How can parents make it clear that the children are not the cause of the separation? What harm is there if they do feel they are to blame?

6. What are the symptoms of depression in a child? What can the parents do about it?

Chapter 6: The Creative Power of Rootedness

1. A father said, "I don't want my kids to have anything to do with that family (the children's mother's family). We don't talk about it, and I see to it there is nothing here to remind them!" What are some of the things that can happen as a result of that?

2. List at least three ways either parent can help the children understand their family legacy (from both sides of their parentage).

3. Rod McKuen spent the remainder of his adult life looking for some trace of his unknown father after his mother's death. Why do children as they grow to adulthood want to know about their parents?

4. Should a parent put down the other parent's family? To what extent should children be expected to evaluate their heritage themselves?

5. How can parents help children adjust to new habits and customs after the separation, particularly around major holidays?

6. What is the value of a parent writing a complete journal of the child's life and presenting it to the young adult child?

Chapter 7: Noncustodial Parenting

1. "Since their mother won the custody, I have no responsibility—except to send a monthly check!" What are the fallacies in that statement?

2. How can the noncustodial parent prevent every visiting day from becoming "circus day" or "Santa Claus Day"?

3. List the ways a noncustodial parent can keep in touch

with the children without seeming to compete with the custodial parent.

4. Should the children dictate the activities or nonactivities (glued to TV) on visiting day? What reasons do you give?

5. Is it worth the trouble for the noncustodial parent to have contact with the children's school? What values are involved in this?

6. What are some of the stumbling blocks in the child's relationship with the noncustodial parent?

Chapter 8: Standing Room

1. "I feel that I have to sacrifice my own interests in order to give the children the break they deserve." What happens when the parent gives up everything for the sake of the children?

2. What are the significant, nonverbal lessons, the children learn from the way the parent conducts himself or herself? Why is it important that the parent make a claim to what the parent is entitled?

3. In what sense does the experience of separation deepen and personalize religious faith?

4. Read Psalm 139. How does this seem to relate to the experience following separation and divorce?

5. Is it selfish and therefore sinful of me to seek satisfaction and enjoyment for myself?

6. How is a sense of self-worth related to good parenting?

Chapter 9: Dating and the Children

1. "It would hurt the children too much if I started dating." What is the truth and the untruth of that statement?

2. There is a grieving time in separation just as there is in death. What is the danger of extending that indefinitely? What are the signs of healing?

3. "Do I have to compromise my standards in order to have companionship?" How would you answer that question?

4. What if the young children cry and put on an act if they see I am going on a date? Should I hide my dating from them?

5. How should I respond to my teenage daughters when they say, "Oh, Mother, be modern. Let him stay overnight!"?

Chapter 10: If You Marry Again

1. In considering remarriage, what is the difference between "taking the children into account" and "letting the children make the adult decision"?

2. What are the dangers implied in this statement: "You will discipline the children—after all, they are yours, not mine!"?

3. A woman told her new husband: "I want you to be a parent to them, but they will not understand if you assume authority over them." What are the issues involved here?

4. What is an appropriate response of the parent and stepparent when a child blurts out that the stepparent is not the real parent and "I don't have to listen to you!"?

5. What are the steps for building a new family life together? What are the dangers? How can the principle of "something old, something new" be utilized?

6. Is it possible to be a good parent even without pretending to be the father or the mother? What kind of agreement is needed to make this effective?

7. What's wrong with the statement: "I don't want to get married, but the children need a father"?

8. What are the values of prenuptial financial agreements in regard to protecting the rights of the children?

Chapter 11: Go for It!

1. Ask yourself what you really want for this next stage of your life. List the steps you can take to move toward that goal. What stops you?

2. Take stock of yourself: your strengths, the skills you have acquired during this period of coping, and the potential you have for the future.

3. Consider the positive aspects of taking some risk compared to being willing to remain in the status quo.

4. Are the chief hindrances to personal advance factors outside yourself or from within yourself?

Selected Bibliography

For Preschool and Early Elementary School Children

Goff, Beth, *Where Is Daddy? The Story of Divorce*. Boston: Beacon Press, 1969.

Hazen, B. S. *Two Homes to Live In: A Child's-Eye View of Divorce*. New York: Human Services Sciences Press, Inc., 1978.

Magid, Ken, and Schreibman, Walt, *Divorce Is . . . A Kid's Coloring Book*. El Toro, Calif.: Penguin Books, 1980.

Sinberg, Janet, *Divorce Is a Grown Up Problem*. New York: Avon Books, 1978.

Stanek, Muriel, *I Won't Go Without a Father*. Chicago: Albert Whitman and Co., 1972.

Stenson, Janet Sinberg, *Now I Have a Step-Parent, and It's Kind of Confusing*. New York: Avon Books, 1979.

For Upper Elementary, Junior High, and Senior High School Children

Blue, Rose, *A Month of Sundays*. New York: Franklin Watts, Inc., 1972.

Blume, Judy, *It's Not the End of the World.* New York: Bradbury Press, Inc., 1972.

Gardner, Richard A., *The Boys and Girls Book About Divorce.* New York: Bantam Books, Inc., 1971.

LeShan, Eda, *What's Going to Happen to Me?: When Parents Separate or Divorce.* New York: Scholastics, Inc., 1978.

Mann, Peggy, *My Daddy Lives in a Downtown Hotel.* New York: Doubleday & Co., Inc., 1973.

Richards, Arlene and Willis, Irene, *How to Get It Together When Your Parents Are Coming Apart.* New York: Bantam Books, Inc., 1977.

For Parents

Atkin, Edith, and Rubin, Estelle, *Part-Time Father.* New York: Vanguard Press, Inc., 1976.

Boszormenyl-Nagy, Ivan and Spark, Geraldine, *Invisible Loyalties.* New York: Harper & Row, Publishers, Inc., 1973.

Burnett, Barbara A., *Everywoman's Legal Guide: Protecting Your Rights at Home, in the Workplace, and in the Marketplace.* New York: Doubleday & Co., Inc., 1983.

Carter, Velma T., and Leavenworth, J. Lynn, *Putting the Pieces Together.* Valley Forge: Judson Press, 1977.

Despert, J. Louis, *Children of Divorce.* New York: Doubleday & Co., Inc., 1953.

Duncan, Roger T., and Duncan, Darlene, *You're Divorced, but Your Children Aren't.* Englewood Cliffs, N.J.: Prentice-Hall, Inc., 1979.

Fromm, Erich, *Art of Loving: An Enquiry into the Nature of Love.* New York: Harper & Row, Publishers, Inc., 1956.

Galper, Miriam, *Co-Parenting: Sharing Your Child Equally.* Philadelphia: Running Press, 1978.

Gardner, Richard, *The Parents Book About Divorce.* New York: Doubleday & Co., Inc., 1977.

Gordon, Thomas, *P.E.T. in Action.* New York: Wyden Books, 1976.

Olson, Richard P., and Della-Pia-Terry, Carole, *Help for Remarried Couples and Families.* Valley Forge: Judson Press, 1983.

Roman, Mel, and Raley, Patricia E., *The Indelible Family.* New York: Rawson, Wade Publishers, Inc., 1980.

Rosenbaum, Jean and Veryl, *Step-parenting*. New York: E. P. Dutton, Inc.

Salk, Lee, *What Every Child Would Like Parents to Know About Divorce*. New York: Harper & Row, Publishers, Inc., 1978.

Tavris, Carol, *Anger: The Misunderstood Emotion*. New York: Simon & Schuster, Inc., 1983.

Thodes, Sonya, and Wilson, Josleen, *Surviving Family Life*. New York: Rawson, Wade Publishers, Inc., 1980.

Turow, Rita, *Daddy Doesn't Live Here Anymore*. New York: Doubleday & Co., Inc., 1978.

Wells, Ronald V., *Spiritual Disciplines for Everyday Living*. Schenectady: Character Research Press, 1982.

Appendix
Tips for Fast Breakfasts
and Portable Lunches

Hardly anyone enjoys the task of making lunches five days a week, trying to come up with something interesting, nutritious, economical, and above all *easy* to prepare. The other problem for working parents is to be able to get something into their children's tummies when they oversleep or take too much time getting ready and then have no time to eat.

We are including some ideas we like which we found in a great cookbook called *The Bean Sprout*, written by Mary B. Kurtz and published by Bergen Creek Publications, Steamboat Springs, Colorado.

Use these ideas to swap with other parents to make your work easier and more productive. One creative mother we know includes in each lunch bag some cartoons or jokes she cuts out of magazines, and her children are always reporting how many of their friends wait to see what is in their lunch. This practice makes them feel very special. If she has a day without a joke or cartoon, they let her know about it. Sometimes she just includes a little note that says, "I love you." That's not too shabby an idea!

Breakfast for a Sleepyhead*
Or Breakfast on the Run

The Encore

An apple, cored and stuffed with peanut butter or cream cheese.

The Banana Split

A banana sliced lengthwise; spread half with peanut butter and top with remaining half.

The Odd Couple

A small bag of granola accompanied by a hard-boiled egg.

The King's Treat

Toast, spread with cream cheese or cottage cheese, topped with preserves, chopped fruit, or nuts.

Brunch

A fried egg sandwich or a peanut butter and jelly sandwich.

Cream 'n' Crunch

A carton of yogurt and some graham crackers.

An Early Freeze

A fruit shake made in a blender with yogurt, milk, an ice cube or two, and your favorite fruit.

The One-Hander

A flour tortilla spread with peanut butter, topped with preserves or banana slices, all rolled up.

A Small Feast

Your choice of fruit, joined by cheese and crackers.

Extras

All the above can be accompanied by a small can of juice, a wet paper towel in a small plastic bag for cleanup, and instructions for throwing away throwaways!

*From *The Bean Sprout*, by Mary B. Kurtz (Steamboat Springs, Colo.: Bergen Creek Publications, 1981), p. 33. Used by permission.

Tips on Brown Baggin' It*

1. In planning alternatives to processed and prepackaged foods for lunch:

   —Think *fresh*. Include fresh, whole-grain breads, fresh fruits, fresh juices or milk, and fresh vegetables.

   —Prepare something *homemade*. As a result you can control the amount of sweetener and the quality of the ingredients, all without additives. Read the label on almost any commercial cookie box, and you will be convinced that you can do a better job and your "TLC" will be a valuable addition.

   —Read *labels*. Be a discriminating shopper.

2. Expand the lunch menu by using a widemouthed thermos for soups, stews, or casseroles. Warm the thermos with hot water before using.

3. Keep cold things cold and hot things hot!

4. Pack desserts that will keep well and are not extremely fragile.

5. Include small cans of juices which have been frozen. They will keep the lunch cool and will be defrosted by lunchtime. Be sure the fruit juices you are using are 100 percent fruit juice. Many "fruit drinks" contain very little real fruit juice.

6. Make up sandwiches in large quantities and freeze them. They will thaw by lunchtime.

7. A wet washcloth or paper towel can be packed in a plastic bag for cleanup.

8. QUICK LUNCH ITEMS

   —Core an apple and stuff it with cream cheese or peanut butter.

   —Split a banana lengthwise, spread it with peanut butter, and cover with the other half; sprinkle with lemon juice.

   —For easy-to-handle fruit, cut up fruit into cubes or chunks and include with yogurt as a dip. Vegetables can be handled the same way by cutting into chunks or sticks.

   —Tortillas can be filled with egg salad, tuna salad, cheese and sprouts, or any favorite peanut butter combination.

   —For a special treat or surprise, use a cookie cutter to cut

Ibid., pp. 43-44. Used by permission.

out identical shapes from slices of bread. Spread with your choice of filling and close.

—Cream cheese can be made into a variety of spreads by adding raisins, dates, nuts, jams, chopped turkey, chopped olives, or any other favorite thing.

—Pita bread can hold just about anything one desires: chopped chicken and salsa, tuna salad with apples, peanut butter and bananas, or egg and yogurt salad.

DATE DUE
